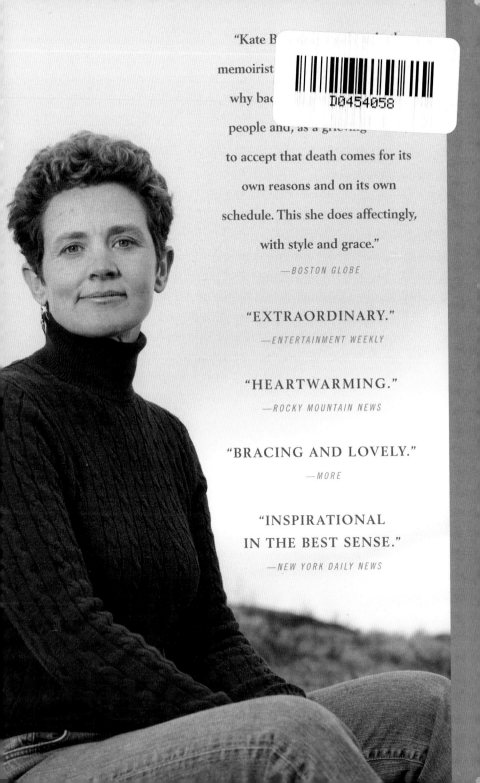

"Kate B_____ memoirist _____ why bac_____ people and, as a g_____ to accept that death comes for its own reasons and on its own schedule. This she does affectingly, with style and grace."

—*BOSTON GLOBE*

"EXTRAORDINARY."

—*ENTERTAINMENT WEEKLY*

"HEARTWARMING."

—*ROCKY MOUNTAIN NEWS*

"BRACING AND LOVELY."

—*MORE*

"INSPIRATIONAL
IN THE BEST SENSE."

—*NEW YORK DAILY NEWS*

Acclaim for Kate Braestrup's

Here If You Need Me

Selected by Time, *the* Washington Post, Rocky Mountain
News, Christian Science Monitor, *and* Newsday
as one of the year's best books

Winner of the Barnes & Noble Discover Award
for best nonfiction book of the year

"*Here If You Need Me* can be read as a superbly crafted memoir of
love, loss, grief, hope, and the complex subtleties of faith. Or it
can be read as the journey of a strong-minded, warmhearted
woman through tragedy to grace.... [Braestrup is] remarkable,
steady, peaceful, and wise." —Jane Ciabattari, *Washington Post*

"Scenes of search-and-rescue as gripping as any police thriller
are juxtaposed with tender, revealing sketches of domestic life
in a family shaken but not shattered by sorrow. On the job,
Braestrup serves as a comforting sounding board for men and
women in a stressful profession. While they search, she rescues,
holding everyone together with her warmhearted common
sense." —Amanda Heller, *Boston Globe*

"Braestrup has fulfilled her mission to tell her—and her husband's—unusual story in a loving and captivating way."
—Jacqueline Blais, *USA Today*

"Extraordinary. Braestrup writes with affecting gravity about
the everyday horrors she encounters. This witty, middle-aged
Maine minister has a calm, earthy authority all her own."
—Jennifer Reese, *Entertainment Weekly*

"A must-read for any parent who has tried to answer a child's hard
questions or for anyone who has struggled to find meaning. Best of
all, this remarkable true story is told with uncommon candor,
grace, and humor.... This is one search-and-rescue you won't
want to miss." —Martha White, *Christian Science Monitor*

"Bracing and lovely. . . . It's hard to imagine a better companion with whom to sit out an agonizing wait or study the lessons of loss and a self-mended heart."   —Martha Fay, *More*

"A simply told, often funny true story about the transformative power of faith."   —*Redbook*

"Beautiful and brave."   —*Glamour*

"Kate Braestrup writes movingly, and with humor, about how she coped when her state trooper husband died in a car crash—by taking on a mission that she never imagined."
        —*Reader's Digest*

"A poignant, funny book by a sympathetic, likable, immensely appealing figure."   —*Booklist*

"Even the most jaded secularist would fall for the chaplain of the Maine Warden Service."
        —Karen Schechner, *Cleveland Plain Dealer*

"So rich in warmth and humanity. . . . A graceful parable of what can happen when human beings stand side by side, steadfast and strong for one another in times of trouble and joy."
        —Susan Larson,
        New Orleans Times-Picayune

"For Braestrup, comforting others becomes a way to heal her own grief, and her spiritual journey is a moving part of this wry, intelligent memoir."
        —Maura Christopher, *Ladies Home Journal*

"Inspirational in the best sense. . . . *Here If You Need Me* resounds with one woman's belief that caring is sacred and helping is holy."   —Sherryl Connelly, *Daily News*

"Cheerful and sure, this chatty, breezy little book is a soothing balm."   —Sarah Peasley, *Rocky Mountain News*

"An honest, endearing account of a life rerouted after devastating loss. . . . Braestrup knows how to tell a good story—the angel is in the details."
        —Kimberly Marlowe Hartnett, *Seattle Times*

Here If You Need Me

A TRUE STORY

Kate Braestrup

BACK BAY BOOKS
Little, Brown and Company
New York   Boston   London

Back Bay Books / Little, Brown and Company
Hachette Book Group USA
237 Park Avenue, New York, NY 10017
Visit our Web site at www.HachetteBookGroupUSA.com

Originally published in hardcover by Little, Brown and Company,
August 2007
First Back Bay paperback edition, July 2008

Back Bay Books is an imprint of Little, Brown and Company. The Back Bay
Books name and logo are trademarks of Hachette Book Group USA, Inc.

Excerpt from "Hand in My Pocket" by Alanis Morissette. Copyright
Universal MCA Music Publishing.

Library of Congress Cataloging-in-Publication Data
Braestrup, Kate.
    Here if you need me : a true story / Kate Braestrup.—1st ed.
      p. cm.
    ISBN 978-0-316-06630-3 (hc) / 978-0-316-06631-0 (pb) /
         978-0-316-04295-6 (special edition)
    1. Braestrup, Kate.   2. Authors, American—20th century—
Biography.   3. Widows—Maine—Biography.   4. Search and rescue
operations—Maine.   I. Title.
PS3552.R246Z46   2007
813'.54—dc22   2006024441

10 9 8 7 6

RRD-IN

Designed by Nancy Singer Olaguera

Printed in the United States of America

AUTHOR'S NOTE

Bangor Theological Seminary, where I trained for the ministry, requires that master's of divinity students study one of the two biblical languages, Hebrew or Greek.

I chose Greek for no particular reason, but my more orthodox classmates approached the class with eager anticipation. They wanted to read the Gospels in the original. Secrets masked by translators of suspect skill and motivation would be revealed, and they would know what the Good News really consisted of. They would know what Jesus *really* said.

What we discovered was what anyone who tries to translate one language into another discovers: many words have no precise cognate. Moreover, a Greek word often has more than one possible cognate in English, sometimes half a dozen or more. Using one rather than another yields subtly or sometimes wildly different meanings. Thus, the assiduous study of Greek offered explanations of but, alas, no resolution to the discrepancies that exist between biblical translations. In short, we students of Greek learned what so many before us had also learned: the Word is a slippery thing.

My favorite example is the word *word* itself. The Gospel of John begins: Ἐν ἀρχῇ ην ὁ λόγος ("In the beginning was the Word"). There's a reason this translation is so common: it's a good and reasonable one, given that English doesn't really have a word that means precisely what λόγος, or Logos, means. Still, there are other, equally plausible cognates for Logos, including *discourse, speech, message, theory, motive, reason, wisdom,* and—my personal favorite—*story:* In the beginning was the *story,* and the *story* was with God, and the *story* was God.

A minister in the Christian tradition must give voice to the Logos: she is a teller of stories. On the other hand, as an ordained minister and a chaplain to the Maine Warden Service, it is my sacred obligation to maintain the confidentiality of the game wardens and the citizens I serve. The roles of confessor and storyteller are in tension.

I have attempted to resolve the tension between confidentiality and storytelling in this book by renaming most of the game wardens, other law enforcement professionals, and ordinary citizens, and by altering significant details of gender, appearance, and life circumstance to render them unrecognizable. Maine is a state of small towns, where everyone knows everyone and everything, so I have taken liberties with the geographic locations and details of events so as to further protect privacy.

*　　*　　*

Along with four small children, three hairy dogs, a life insurance policy, assorted size 10½ shoes, and a set of iron barbells I cannot lift, I have inherited the bulk of my late husband's Logos, or story. A marriage, willy-nilly, requires you to trust that your spouse will tell your story truthfully and lovingly when you are no longer around to tell it yourself. I hope I haven't betrayed Drew's implicit trust in me by how I have represented him here.

May my children, Zachary, Peter, Ellie, and Woolie, be merciful in their eventual refutations, literary or otherwise, of what I have written about them. More important, may they discern my affection from this and from all their mother's imperfect works.

Here If You
Need Me

Chapter One

A six-year-old girl has wandered off from a family picnic near Masquinongy Pond, and she remains missing after a long day of waiting. The Maine Warden Service has mounted a search. There are dozens of people combing the woods near the picnic grounds. Some are local guys, volunteers from the community, but most of them are game wardens in green uniforms. Handlers from the warden service K-9 unit have brought dogs trained to find people, and dogs—those braced in the bows of boats drifting over the surface of the pond's marshy edge—trained to alert to the signature scent of a cadaver.

The parents may or may not know about the cadaver dogs. They may or may not realize that when Chief Warden Pilot Charlie Later's plane buzzes overhead, he is scanning the brown bed of the pond for a small, pale human shape beneath the water.

The parents do know this much: they love their child,

and their child wanders in an inhospitable environment. They know the dark is coming on. They have been told that the Maine Warden Service chaplain has been called. What else could this be about but death?

Around three in the afternoon, as my kids are trooping into the kitchen, dumping their backpacks in the mudroom, describing their school days, the telephone rings.

"Your Holiness!" Lieutenant Trisdale roars. "We've got a situation up here by Masquinongy Pond we could use your help with."

So by four, I am waiting by Chickawaukee Lake. Lieutenant Trisdale has sent a seaplane to fetch me. The lake is a ten-minute drive from my house, so I had time to eat a bowlful of supper's chicken stew and to swallow a Dramamine. I have heard that Charlie Later takes a dim view of wardens who puke in his airplane, and I don't want to test his tolerance.

My car is parked in the little lot adjoining what passes for a beach, a mud bank that the city of Rockland improves in summertime with sand and a lifeguard. If this were summer, there would be children paddling in the shallows, canoes and kayaks on the water, and—increasingly—"personal watercraft," or jet skis, zooming around.

But it is late October. The lake, abandoned save for a small flock of migrating mallards, is a placid gray mirror for the autumn afternoon. The sky boasts an archipelago of clouds so perfect in their imitation of islands that in the lee of the largest one, I can make out an inlet where a boat might find secure anchorage.

I blow on my hands and tuck them into the scratchy woolen armpits of my uniform jacket. I've forgotten my gloves.

People hear *warden service* and assume I am a prison chaplain. They picture me at the Supermax, counseling rapists and accompanying the Dead Man Walking to the electric chair. "Maine doesn't have the death penalty," I explain, and in any case, I work with game wardens, not prison wardens. Game wardens are law enforcement officers who work under the Maine Department of Inland Fisheries and Wildlife. Finding a lost child in the woods is among the many useful things these folks know how to do.

How old a child? "A little girl," the lieutenant had said. Unavoidably, the image of my youngest daughter, age eight, comes to me. Her name is Anne, but her nickname is Woolie, with manifold familial variations (Woolie-Bully, Wooglet, Woo), and her cheek was warm and soft against my mouth when I kissed her good-bye.

I dial my house to hear my children's voices. There are four altogether. Zachary is the eldest, at fourteen, and the rest follow in reasonably tidy, two-year intervals: Peter is twelve, Ellie is ten, Woolie is eight. "I know. You would think we'd *planned* them," their father would say, deadpan, when others expressed surprise (or was it dismay?) at the monotonous regularity with which he and I had reproduced.

Woolie answers the telephone with a complaint prepared: Peter has gone off with the electric pencil sharpener. He won't give it back, and he called Woolie a bastard. Such language is insulting and morally wrong. In addition, it's inaccurate, and I wonder whether this should be an aggravating factor in my adjudication.

"All right, Woogie-Piggie, I'll talk to him.

"Peter, share the pencil sharpener," I tell him when he comes on the line. "And no cursing."

"Okay," says Peter cheerfully. I can hear Woolie shrieking insults in the background. "Peace, Mom-Dude."

It's early in the search. There's hope—real hope, not the faint hope that families cling to as days drag on.

By now I know not to bother anticipating or planning for these calls. Hope and grief make a habit of presenting themselves in novel ways every time, and what is required in the way of a tender and appropriate response changes every time as well. It does an anxious family no good at all to have the chaplain arrive worn out with worry or projecting her own parental feelings onto a loss that does not belong to her.

"Incidents can be rated on a scale of one to ten," a Denver, Colorado, police detective once told me. "Sometime during your career, you might get one or two incidents worth a ten. A bad murder, maybe a young victim, or you shoot somebody, or maybe go through the death of a friend and fellow officer. Those are tens. Most incidents are going to be way down on the scale, like maybe a two or a three. But you know what? I think it's all those little twos, threes, and fours that add up over time. I think those are the ones that get you in the end."

By my lights, a one is when they find the lost person alive. Ones are good. A ten is—well, a ten is a dead warden, I suppose. Still, line-of-duty deaths are rare, if not quite rare enough. (The Maine Warden Service has the highest number of line-of-duty deaths of any agency in the state, a total of fourteen in the 125 years of the service's existence.)

Where is the Masquinongy Pond search going to fall on that Colorado detective's scale of one to ten? If the child is dead, it's going to be up there around seven or eight for all the wardens as well as for me.

Peace.

My children are all alive and well, if not well behaved. I can count on a solid little hit of adrenaline to clear my head when I arrive on scene. So I kick idly at the gravel, take some deep breaths, blow on my hands, wonder whether Peter and Woolie's issues merit intervention by a shrink, fantasize idly about sailing to the islands in the sky.

Those ducks had better get a wiggle on; winter is definitely on its way. There are ice crystals forming around the woody stems of the cattails. Turtles, their metabolisms slowed to geologic speed, have hunkered down in the mud for six months of cold coma. It won't be long before the surface of the lake freezes into a solid pane of ice, and anyone who wants to walk on water can. By January it will be thick enough to drive a truck onto, in theory at least. (Every few years, the dive team is called out to retrieve the body of a driver whose estimate of the ice's thickness proved tragically inaccurate.) When the ice is that thick, I'll be willing to let my children skate, maybe.

Right now, my four children are sitting at the kitchen table, eating the cookies they were supposed to save for after supper, doubtless still arguing over the pencil sharpener or, if they've finished with that, arguing over which video they will watch tonight if Mom is still away and unable to enforce the "no videos on school nights" rule.

"It would be nice if this little girl turns out to be alive," I suggest out loud.

Barely audible at first, above the adenoidal agreement of the ducks, a faint buzz grows steadily louder. The warden service seaplane suddenly pops up above the high blueberry barrens at the far end of the lake. Its appearance breaks the island illusion; the clouds are clouds again. The plane gives a friendly wing-waggle and swings toward the water. It is aimed at the wrong shore, but I know by now not to jump and wave. The pilot has to land the plane nose into the wind. When the pontoons have made contact, flinging up twin plumes of white spray and carving sleigh tracks in the lake's silvery surface, Charlie will turn the plane around, and it will grumble gently to my shore.

Once I'm installed in the passenger seat, Charlie drives

the plane hard into the wind, the pontoons skid off the water, and we ascend over the peak of Ragged Mountain.

"The lieutenant is going to meet us at Masquinongy Pond," Charlie says. "I guess it's not looking so good."

I nod, looking carefully out the window at distant objects to forestall nausea. Penobscot Bay lies to our right, gleaming blackish blue around the shreds of land that form Islesboro, Northaven, Vinalhaven, Isle au Haut, and myriad little islands. I can pick out details: Owl's Head Light, the breakwater in Rockland Harbor, the square hull of the ferry backing out of the slip at Lincolnville Beach. Old mountains, smoothed by glaciers and time, roll off to the north and west. Charlie turns westward and flies behind the sun.

Charlie's hands rest lightly on the plane's steering wheel. I have an identical yoke in front of my seat that tilts in tandem with his as Charlie makes small adjustments to the variable air. Charlie's father was a warden service pilot too. Charlie grew up flying all over the state, and his relationship with an airplane seems at least as natural as my relationship with my feet.

And so, though I am prone to motion sickness of all varieties, I do like flying with Charlie. I like to look at Maine from this new angle and from the sky rediscover its familiar features—seacoast, church spires, winding roads, huge tracts of forest, silver lakes, trailer parks, rolling meadows. The tree-lined edges of the pastures below us are accented with a startling yellow, as if a giant artist used his thumb to smudge the vivid dust of a pastel landscape. It takes me a little time to realize that the dusty smudge is where the fallen yellow leaves of the maples have drifted.

"It's harder when it's a child," Charlie is saying, and I remember again the warmth of my daughter's cheek.

The parents of the missing girl are standing, stage lit, within a cone of lamplight at the far end of the Masquinongy Pond Recreation Area parking lot. Insects whirl drunkenly above their heads, and among them I note the disconcerting, flitting motion of little brown myotis bats taking their evening meal.

Perhaps thirty yards away, a modified RV belonging to the Salvation Army casts its own circle of light and supports its own rave of light-drugged insects, its own dance of bats. Through the open back door of the vehicle, I can see Brian Clark, a plump, walleyed veteran of many search scenes, washing pots. He will have spent a long afternoon cheerfully dishing up coffee, doughnuts, and Dinty Moore beef stew to search crews as they came in from the woods. Most of the volunteer searchers have reluctantly gone home for now. In the darkness, they can do no more than spread their scent, contaminating the area that the K-9s will continue searching through the night.

"I'm Reverend Braestrup," I announce. "I'm the chaplain for the Maine Warden Service."

"Ralph Moore," the child's father says. "This is my wife Marian. We're not churchgoers." The woman smiles apologetically as if I might have been offended by her husband's abrupt tone.

"I'm not a church minister." I shrug and smile. His face does not relinquish its skepticism, but Mr. Moore tugs once on my proffered hand, like a man testing the strength of a knot.

"Actually, I should probably tell you: we're atheists."

"Ah."

"No offense."

"I'm not offended," I say. "What a long, hard day you two have had."

"Yes," he says.

"I'm so sorry this has happened to you."

Mr. Moore looks away, toward the edge growth that fringes the parking lot. "I am too."

Mrs. Moore stands still, but her eyes scan constantly for signs from the surrounding darkness, her arms wrapped tightly across her chest. It's work to wait this way, aching physical labor.

"It's miserable to wait," I observe, and she nods, still scanning, her mouth taut.

Beyond the parking lot, the edge growth gives way to mixed deciduous woodland that rolls on for miles, interrupted only by an occasional swamp or swiftly flowing stream. It's been nine hours since the family dog returned and Alison did not. The Moores are tourists on vacation from a large Massachusetts city, but even if they were locals, the forest and the nearby bog and water would seem increasingly menacing as the hours wore on past mealtime, past bedtime. The people with uniforms, guns, and dogs had arrived in their emergency vehicles, blue lights flashing, as well as airplanes and boats, verifying the seriousness of what is, the awful plausibility of what might be.

"Look, Reverend," Mr. Moore says, gesturing into the darkness. "I know all these guys have to keep looking. I can tell they are putting on a brave face for Marian here. But you can tell me the truth."

Unbeliever though he may be, Mr. Moore is not asking the lady in the clerical collar for an objective assessment of a practical situation. He wants the God's honest truth. He wants me to tell him, with all the weight and authority my presence conveys, that his daughter is not dead.

"Do you think she's dead?" I asked Lieutenant Trisdale after Charlie Later landed me safely on Masquinongy Pond. We were driving to the search scene in his truck, bouncing over the old roads, the lieutenant's paperwork, coffee cups, and collection of cell phones leaping about my knees. Fritz Trisdale has nearly three decades of experience behind his assessment. Whatever he says, I will believe.

Fritz scrubbed thoughtfully at the five o'clock shadow on his jaw. "I'll tell you what, your Reverendship," he said slowly. "I think she's still okay, to be honest with you. It's not like the kid was retarded or suicidal or something. She's just good and lost. Those woods have been cut over so many times that there's plenty of scrub and low growth to keep her hidden from us. Hell, you'd practically have to step on someone to find 'em in there. She's probably scared of the voices she hears, if she hears 'em at all. I think she's alive. Ronnie Dunham's bringing his dog Grace up this evening, and Grace'll have a fresh nose." Fritz stopped and gave it another thought but came to the same conclusion. "Yeah," he said. "I think we're going to find her."

"Listen," the child's father is saying to me. "I'm an engineer. I work with statistics. You don't have to bullshit me."

His wife is holding onto my hand, tightly, and her hand is cold. She turns her eyes to me as her husband continues: "I know that the longer this search goes on, the greater the chances are that my little girl is dead." Mrs. Moore flinches sharply at the word, and grips my hand even more firmly. Later my knuckles will ache, and I'll find the marks of her fingernails in my palm.

"I have been on many searches with the wardens," I answer him. "These guys are good at what they do. They have a lot of experience between them. And I've been with them on searches where they really don't think they are going to find somebody alive."

I pause and both parents lean closer, as if my voice might suddenly soften beyond the reach of their ears, but I speak boldly. "If the wardens have told you that in their professional opinion they think they will find your daughter alive, I believe we're going to do just that."

Mr. Moore's knees visibly wobble. Mrs. Moore gives forth

with a weak exclamation, and her hand softens in mine. *Oh, please, Jesus, let this be true. Let the little girl be alive.*

If it isn't true, then one of the searchers will find the body. It is a small body to begin with, no more than fifty-five pounds according to the report, and it will have dwindled in death. There will be no vital signs, no spring of skin or tapping pulse beneath the warden's gentle fingers at wrist or throat, no warmth. The clothing will correspond to the description each searcher carries: khaki pants, light blue jacket, blue sweatshirt with a picture of Elmo on the front, gym socks, and Teva sandals.

"I wish we had better news for you," the lieutenant will have to say to the parents. "Oh, I am so sorry," I will say. And the wardens will make their assessments of the scene, consider the possibility of foul play, take measurements and photographs, note the condition of the body, call the medical examiner, inform the news media. When the medical examiner authorizes removal, they will place the little body in a body bag and carry it from the woods. Then they will go home, hold the warm, living bodies of their own children, and know too well the risk they take by loving in such a precarious world.

At eight forty-five, Alison still has not been found. The Moores and I are sitting in a little row on a picnic table, our feet braced on the seat. We are on a first-name basis by this time; they have dispensed with "Reverend," and I have been invited to call them Ralph and Marian. I'm secretly pleased to note that Marian is no longer holding my hand, and Ralph is no longer keeping his distance from her fear or from my comfort. Husband and wife sit close to one another, their hands entwined, and close to me.

Over our heads, the bats continue darting in their unnerving, skittish flights. The Moores tell me the story of their last vacation day, of their cheerful plan for a final autumn picnic, about the thermos full of hot chowder, the crisp Macoun apples they picked at an orchard the day before. They need to describe the way the dog ran off and the little girl went after him, calling his name, and how they didn't think to follow her.

I explain again how the warden service conducts a search and how seldom they fail to find what they are looking for, even in less-accessible terrain. Mr. Moore likes it when I refer to "statistical profiles of lost juveniles" and use initialisms like PLS (point last seen). He wants to hear about the search protocols, the reasons why the search is being concentrated in one area rather than another, why the search planes stopped flying at dusk, whether and how he and Marian should speak with the television news crews slated to appear at dawn. He takes up my suggestion about sipping water and reminds his wife to stay hydrated.

Marian breaks in at intervals: "Should I have followed her?" "Wouldn't a good mother have known something was wrong before her baby got so far away that even all these men with planes and dogs can't find her?"

"Aw, darlin'," Ralph says, stroking his wife's back.

"Why can't all these men with planes and dogs find Alison?" Marian asks me.

"It's surprisingly hard to find a small person. These woods are dense. You'd almost have to step right on her to find her."

"But wouldn't she hear us calling to her and answer?" Ralph asks.

Not if she's dead.

"She's asleep," I say.

"Why do you weep?" Jesus inquires of a bereaved crowd in Mark's gospel (5:39). "The child is not dead, but sleeping!"

"Little kids who get lost in the woods do something really smart," I tell Marian. "When they realize they're lost, they find a snug place—like under a bush—curl up, and go to sleep. Adults tend to keep moving; they keep trying to find their own way out. They think they have to solve the problem themselves. Little kids conk out and wait for the grown-ups to solve it. If Alison is under a bush asleep, she probably can't hear us hollering."

Alison's mother looks at me, at my clerical collar and my uniform. She believes me.

I want to be right. I try not to want this too much.

It's quarter past ten. The moon is up, a sliver in the sky with a pale yellow halo of high clouds.

The picnic, the dog scampering into the forest, Alison's blue-clad back disappearing between the trees—a sharpened image her mother fears she will carry forever as the last. The

Moores are telling me the story again. They describe their initial attempts to find their daughter, the half-embarrassed cell-phone call to 911, the arrival of a sheriff's deputy and then a game warden who initiated the search that now proceeds outward from the PLS according to statistical best bets. The volunteers came and then the K-9 teams, and a Salvation Army van, and a chaplain with her God's honest truth.

Why do you weep? Your daughter is not dead, but sleeping!

"Jesus took the child by the hand and said to her, 'Talitha cum,' which means, 'Little girl, get up!' And immediately the girl got up and began to walk about" (Mark 5:41). That's how the gospel story goes.

That is the way the Moores' story will go when they get back to the city. It is a story to be filed away for graduations, for Alison's wedding rehearsal supper, and for her own children: "Once upon a time, Alison got lost . . ."

And this is how the Maine Warden Service found her: At about three o'clock in the morning, a few miles almost due west of the PLS, Warden Ron Dunham's K-9, Grace, found a little girl in an Elmo sweatshirt curled up under some brush.

Ron hunkered down and let the dog's cold nose awaken her. "Hey, honey," Ron said gently. "Do you want to go home?"

The girl sat up and rubbed her eyes. "Yes," she said calmly. She crawled out from her nesting place and got to her feet.

"Want me to carry you?"

"No, thank you," Alison said politely.

Alison's nice manners would be part of the story too, for Ron Dunham as well as for her parents. Gazing fondly at her and at each other, the Moores would tell the tale: " 'No, thank you,' she said. Can you believe it?"

"Want me to hold your hand?" Ron asked.

The child considered for a moment. "Yes," she decided.

So Warden Dunham and Alison come walking out of the woods hand in hand, past the Salvation Army food wagon and into the parking lot, with K-9 Grace trotting proudly ahead. And my whole, lovely job at that moment was to bear witness to rejoicing and to join in the gladness of the coming day.

Chapter Two

Wth perhaps another fifteen years to go before he could retire from his job as a trooper for the Maine State Police, my husband James Andrew "Drew" Griffith was already planning a second career as a Unitarian Universalist minister. He imagined himself serving a church and working as a law enforcement chaplain on the side. He could respond to crime scenes and search scenes, perform death notifications, and help families and officers cope with the spiritual and emotional dimensions of the work he was all too familiar with in his current occupation. Earnest, intelligent, brave, and tender, Drew would have made a great minister.

According to our plan, I would have gone on writing, but I would also be a minister's wife. It would have been a fine life.

One Monday morning in April 1996, my alarm clock went off. My husband grunted, turned over, and reached for me. For a half hour we snoozed entwined, a caduceus of warm, familiar flesh, until the backup alarm clock on his side of the bed rang, the dogs appeared at the bedside, and a child began to stir in the next room.

Two hours after this, the sheets were still tangled and, doubtless, still held the residual heat of his body as well as his scent. Downstairs, where I stood in the kitchen, Drew's cereal bowl was in the sink. White bowl, stainless steel sink. My husband's body, at that moment, lay along the front seat of his cruiser, his crew-cut head resting gently in the crook of his arm, just as if, his friend Tom would later tell me, he had decided to take a nap there, in the lemon-colored sunlight of an April morning.

"I don't know," the sergeant said, when I asked to be taken to the scene to see the body.

In the local paper that very afternoon, there would be photographs showing the smashed Maine State Police cruiser and the back end of a paramedic protruding from the passenger-side door. The front end of the paramedic—Peter Lammert, I know him—was trying to determine what, if anything, could be done to hold my husband's life in his body. There was nothing. The impact of a fully loaded box truck striking the driver's side of a car carries a force that neither the car door nor the body behind it is designed to withstand. By any ordinary measure, Drew died instantly.

Death can be plausibly described as instantaneous, yet our cells have a certain autonomy. Only when the heart is stilled and the blood no longer streams effervescent with oxygen do the cells begin to shut down. It can take a while—six hours or more—for the last cellular outposts to flicker into darkness.

For hours, and only a mile or so from home, Drew's body lay on the driver's seat of his cruiser. One by one, or perhaps in clusters, his cells extinguished themselves. Finally, the driver's side door was cut away from where it held him in a grip both tenacious and tender. The crumpled metal did not bruise him; a little blood showed at the corner of his mouth, but nowhere else, I was told. He was loaded into a hearse and driven to the state medical examiner's lab in Augusta—and by that time it was at last accurate, even on the level of the microscopic, to refer to what was loaded as an "it" and not a "him."

I would go to the bridge only days later. There were skid marks on its asphalt surface. They began precisely where the truck collided with the car. They marked an instant in time as a point in space. When no cars were passing by, it was possible to hear the river, the moving air, the birds. It was possible to stand or place a hand or sink to my knees on that place—amid the fragments of red and clear glass, the flecks of smoky blue paint, the bits of metal—where my husband's life came to an end.

Love begins with the body; the love between Drew and me certainly did, in any case. He was very handsome, although I didn't think so when we first met. He was a photographer then, not yet a police officer. He had a scraggly beard and longish hair. He exercised assiduously, which did not endear him to me. I fancied myself an intellectual at twenty-one and believed attention to one's physique smacked of narcissism. Though riven by the same, stupid combination of vanity and anxiety that most young women are prey to, I pretended an enlightened disinterest in the whole culture of physical perfection. I did not shave my legs. I chopped off my own hair. For Drew's well-developed forearms, ridged abdomen, and the impressive spread of his latissimus dorsi, I had only condescension. In theory, anyway. But when he called to ask if I'd like to see a movie with him, I said yes. This could be described as mere lust, and lust was involved, of course. But *lust* is too diffuse: it will attach itself to punk-rock drummers and English professors and wholly imaginary persons. Its real power is only acquired through specificity: I want not a body, but *this* body, this one here, Drew's body, his scent and heat, his scary strength, his warm mouth.

Once he became a state trooper, Drew's professional life had an intimate physical aspect. He had to do brave and loving things to and with the bodies of others. Take, for example, those he arrested, particularly those who fought back, the ones he would have to wrestle with, the weight of his body pressing them into the ground, his mouth against an ear shouting instructions ("Give it up! Give it up!") as he groped beneath a sweaty belly for hands and weapons. Those bodies smelled of inadequate hygiene and, nearly always, of alcohol. When he had them safely handcuffed, he would help them up and cradle the backs of their heads in his palm so they wouldn't hurt themselves getting into his cruiser. Once he took the tiny hand of an abused four-year-old girl who led him out back, behind her house, to show him where her father had chopped her puppy to pieces with an ax. Drew held the shape of that small hand in his palm for weeks. There were the bodies of those who, on receiving official police notification of a loved one's death, collapsed against his Kevlar-stiffened chest and wept. He would hold them gently and murmur, "That's all right. That's all right."

His body was a tool of his trade, trained to the arcane demands of policing: the holds, takedowns, cuff 'n' stuff, and CPR. So he lifted weights, bicycled, and ran long distances—fast. His arms could press a lot of iron away from his chest. His heart was in superb condition: low blood pressure, cholesterol count in the peachy zone. His body became more beautiful with every passing year, something that after our four babies could not be said of mine. "You will always be beautiful to me," he would tell me, kissing me, and maybe I would have.

He heard the book reviewed on National Public Radio, and so, for my thirty-first birthday, my husband gave me a heavy tome entitled *Death to Dust: What Happens to Dead Bodies?*, by Kenneth V. Iserson, MD. I considered this a wildly romantic gift. Who but Drew would know how entranced I would be by such a book? I spent two weeks immersed in its pages, emerging at intervals to engage him in discussions of funereal arcana: organ donation, embalming, postmortem cosmetics, the expense of coffins and urns, cremation, and so on. Iserson's primary ambition for the book was to increase the number of organ donors by enlightening readers to the impossibility of avoiding the "mutilating" effects of death, which, the claims of the funeral industry notwithstanding, are inevitable even in the most thoroughly embalmed corpse. His secondary theme was that the care of a loved one's dead body was, until very recently, an intimate privilege, one now usurped by professionals.

Modern culture does not encourage us, let alone require us, to take care of the bodies of our dead, any more than we are required to take care of our loved ones as they give birth or suffer or die. Instead, we are offered the expensive illusion that through a mortician's skills the bodies of those we love will remain. There will be roses in their cheeks, chemicals in their systems, and thickly padded coffins to preserve those beloved limbs from the saprophytes that would otherwise claim them. Your loved one will never be dirt, they say.

Iserson recommends resisting this illusion. He advocates giving away undamaged organs to the needy living, and caring for what remains personally—bathing the colorless face, arranging the stiffened limbs, choosing a garment, and dressing the corpse. Dig the hole yourself, if you can. Get the dust and ash on your own hands.

After all, for thousands and thousands of years, ordinary people dealt with their own dead. Why is it that we have not evolved to tolerate and, in some sense, to actively require the experience of personally preparing and burying the bodies of those we love? My father, a former Marine, told me that part of the pledge Marines make is that nobody—no body—is left on the field of battle. *Semper fidelis.* Even the dead are retrieved, sometimes at considerable risk to the living. Why bother to make such a pledge, unless it is desirable that our bodies not fall into the hands of loveless strangers, even after our souls have departed?

"Will you take care of my body when I die?" I shouted to Drew from my chair on the lawn, where I read Dr. Iserson's book and nursed our fourth baby under the willow tree. Drew was setting up the sprinkler for the older children to play in.

"Sure, honey," he answered, and I, like a Marine, felt distinctly braver.

When the funeral director, Mr. Moss, arrived early Tuesday morning, I knew precisely what our preferences were when it came to the disposal of what Mr. Moss gently referred to as "the remains."

I am his remains, I thought.

"You may not embalm him," I said. "Not even a little bit. And no makeup, either. He is to be cremated, and I would like to witness the cremation." Mr. Moss had spread pamphlets and a catalog with pictures of coffins across the dining room table. I did not look at them.

At that moment, Drew's body was being autopsied. Tests for systemic drugs and alcohol were performed, and all, unsurprisingly, came back negative. The chest cavity was opened, his lungs and good stout heart examined, the cause of death confirmed: lacerations to the aorta, to the anterior vestibule of the heart, to the superior vena cava—devastating injuries to all major internal organs, which could not be "harvested." The brain was removed, weighed, examined for defects that might have added complexity to the accident investigation. There were none.

"Drew would have wanted the cheapest possible coffin," I told Mr. Moss, "provided it is also the one that will cremate most completely and with the least environmental impact." The cheapest coffin, which was essentially made of cardboard, turned out, by happy coincidence, to be covered with a nice, state-police-blue fabric.

"That's perfect," I said.

"Good," Mr. Moss replied. "And you want to attend the cremation?"

"Yes," I said. "In addition, I want to bathe and dress his body myself. And I will be the one who closes his coffin for the last time."

"You prefer to, ah, do the dressing and so forth to the body *yourself*," Mr. Moss said carefully, making sure.

"Yes," I said. "I do."

Stainless steel sink, a white bowl, and a stainless spoon, bathed in the lemon yellow light of that morning. I picked up the spoon and put it in my mouth. It tasted of steel and milk. I wanted it to be warm. I wanted it to be Drew.

My son Peter came into the kitchen. I reached for him, but he did not come to me right away. "Maybe Dad has been reincarnated already," he said. His voice was raw, fierce. Peter was seven years old. His father had been dead for two hours. "Maybe Dad is a tiger."

"She wants to bathe and dress the body."

"She wants to *what?*"

"She wants to bathe and dress the body."

"Oh, Jesus. Herself?"

The discussion between the funeral director and higher-ups in the state police went on in this vein late into Tuesday evening and on into Wednesday morning.

What were they afraid of? The same thing I was afraid of. The same thing any of us might be afraid of these days, when birth and death are not "processed" in our homes by our own hands. We have no experience to guide us.

I am quite sure that from the outside my desire to see and to care for my husband's body appeared unshakable. Looking back, I can admit to doubts: *What if my beloved's corpse disgusts me? What if seeing him and touching him make it hurt more?* Yet by instinct as well as by a more intellectual conviction, I knew that I had to walk up to that which would hurt me most: Drew's body without Drew in it. I wanted to do it not because it would help me heal—healing was both indefinable and unimaginable—but because it was the authoritative command of an authentic love. Tuesday night, I lay on Drew's pillow, in his smell, and did not sleep. His body would arrive at the funeral parlor the next morning. *How could it possibly hurt more than this?*

Trooper Tom Ballard came to the house Wednesday morning to tell me that I would be permitted to tend to Drew's body. "They wanted me to talk you out of it," he said soberly. "I told them that I've known you for a long time and that I've never been able to talk you out of or into anything, and neither has anyone else."

"Thank you," I said.

"So they said I should go with you," he continued. "And Sergeant Drake and Sergeant Cunningham are coming with us too."

"All right."

"I'll go too," said my mother.

At the funeral home, the door of the cool, ordinary room was opened, and there he was. He was dead. And I will not lie, he looked dead. But it was comfort, joy, and sweet relief, not horror or pain, to see his body there.

Drew lay on a white-enameled steel table. He had one bruise on his right thigh. He wore the novelty Halloween boxer shorts our son Zachary had chosen for him, and a T-shirt over his chest, which was thickly bandaged. A neat tonsure of staples circled his scalp. His hands rested by his sides.

My husband's smell was at home in our bed, and his white cereal bowl was still in the sink. My husband had an incision in his chest, and the top of his head was held on by staples. My husband left himself three days before, two miles from this cool room. He was gone the instant the red and clear glass was shattering, flying, shining in the air. My husband might already have been reincarnated as a tiger.

My love and Drew's began with latissimus dorsi and the ferocious desire that would have screwed us into one flesh but couldn't. He died. I lived. Like all the very best of loves, it could only have come to this.

Tom, my mother, the two sergeants, and I dressed his body gently in a Class A Maine State Police uniform, crying a little, but laughing a little too. It's absurdly difficult to put clothing onto a body that cannot cooperate, and what was there to do but imagine Drew's amusement at this necessary indignity and laugh with him? Then Sergeant Cunningham tenderly slid those cool, bluish feet into boots shaped to fit exactly. He took the bootlaces between his fingers and tied them into crisp little bows with a practiced gesture that he must use with his own boots. To Drew's jacket, Tom pinned Drew's badge and whistle; he buckled on the belt and bandolier.

I washed Drew's face with a soft, damp cloth. *This is what Drew would have done for me,* I thought. And in all the time that I shall live without him—time roaring and tumbling at me like some merciless, black avalanche—I will be able to tell myself that I bore our love with my own hands all the way to the last hard place. *"Semper fidelis,"* I told him, washing him tenderly around the mouth and jaw and closed eyes, then smoothing his hair with my hand. Leaving the cool room where Drew's body lay was harder than it was to enter it.

CHAPTER THREE

My children, like many other children, attached themselves at a very early age to what child psychologists call "transitional love objects." Drew used to call them *"objets d'amour,"* and the children picked up on it. "I can't go to bed!" Zachary might shout. "I can't find my *objet d'amour!"*

Zach had a stuffed rabbit named Rab-Rab. At least it started out as a rabbit. By the time Zach was three, Rab-Rab had dwindled and flattened into a limp, dingy, only vaguely zoomorphic thing. (Zach still loves him to this day.)

Peter expressed his affection for his handwoven cotton blanket by chewing the long, soft weft threads that pulled easily from the loose weave. We would sometimes find these in his diaper, and, distressingly, hanging halfway out of him. By the time Peter was in preschool, Blankie had been eaten down to the size of a well-loved dishrag.

On the theory that they might want to practice being big brothers when I was pregnant for the third time, I bought a sweet little baby doll in pink jammies for Zachary and Peter. The boys spent a desultory afternoon taping toilet-paper diapers to her and then lost interest. A few months later, their sister was born. Ellie adopted the doll as soon as she was capable of deliberate, empathetic care, which for her was at about two months. At two years, she named the doll Jesus.

Jesus was quite a pretty doll until her infant caregiver inadvertently puked on her head. Jesus came out of the washing machine looking like Don King. Also, her cloth body proved less durable than her plastic head and extremities. Through the ferocity of Ellie's toddler affection, Jesus was eventually transformed into a macabre wind chime of plastic limbs and rags dangling from the doll's still-smiling head.

Even so, Ellie dressed Jesus carefully in her old newborn T-shirts, fed her picnics of shredded leaves and gravel in the backyard, and placed her facedown for her nap, so her wide-open eyes could get a rest from seeing.

"What a *friend* you have in Jesus," her father would comment soberly, as Ellie wheeled Jesus past us in a little plastic stroller. And Ellie would agree, no doubt wondering why her mother was suddenly convulsed with mirth.

Woolie never fixated on an *objet d'amour*. The reason was obvious enough: Woolie was seldom alone. Educated, or perhaps virtually lobotomized by the first three children, I gave up trying to inculcate independence in my youngest child. She nursed for thirty months, was carried constantly, and spent most of her nights sleeping blissfully between her parents, her arms and legs spread wide, somehow managing to claim most of the king-size bed for her own ten-pound infant self. What need had she for a stuffed rabbit, blankie, or dolly? Mama was her transitional love object, her *objet d'amour.* Drew was mine.

In the week before Drew's funeral, while his body still lay at the funeral home, I thought about asking Mr. Moss if I might come over for the night or for just a nap, even. "Couldn't we set up a cot beside Drew in the reception parlor?" I would ask him, in tones of the sweetest reason. "We so seldom slept apart." I could nestle there, beside my dead husband's coffin, concealed and resting easy amid the innumerable bouquets that filled the corner of that vast Victorian room.

Mr. Moss might have gone along with it, for all I know, but I was too chicken to ask. For me, there was no sleep to be had in what was now my own bed. Well, Woolie's and mine.

When my shiny black Belgian sheepdog, Cornelia, was struck and killed by a car, I buried her myself. I was eighteen years old. I dug the hole in that part of my family's property reserved for the interment of beloved pets, lined it with a bed of wildflowers, then placed Cornelia's body on top. With my own hands, I covered her with dirt. To keep animals from disturbing her remains, I gathered rocks from the surrounding fields and woods and piled them atop the grave. Then I stepped back and with a curiously dry eye considered the result. My pile of rocks was just a pile of rocks. That is, it was not as artfully arranged as my faithful Cornelia deserved.

So I pulled apart the pile and began stacking the rocks again, more deliberately this time, with greater care.

The new pile was somewhat more attractive than the first, but it still wasn't quite fine enough. Again, I pulled down the cairn, again I recommenced my labors—all this, I might add, to honor a dog that in life had displayed no interest whatsoever in aesthetics. No matter. I built and rebuilt that pile at least six times. For as long as I was fussily gathering, placing, and judging stones, then casting them aside, I still had a dog. When I placed the last stone on the grave and walked away, my dogless life would commence. It was a moment I desperately wanted to postpone.

I did not bury Drew's body with my own hands. Drew wanted to be cremated. "I want to attend the cremation," I told Mr. Moss.

"All right," he said.

"I shall stay for the whole thing," I said, "beginning to end."

"Of course," said Mr. Moss.

"I'll carry his ashes home myself," I said.

Mr. Moss gently inclined his head in a sort of bow. "Of course," he said again.

I wore a dress Drew liked the day I accompanied his body to the crematory. It was our last date, in a way. Mom came with me, along with Drew's friend Billy, and Drew's father and stepmother.

"What sort of fuel do you use to burn the bodies?" my mother asked Mr. Moss with interest.

Mr. Moss, in his dark suit and shiny shoes, was holding the back of the hearse open while two employees of the Parklawn Memorial Garden unloaded Drew's coffin and placed it on a stainless steel trolley. They grunted with the effort.

Cremating someone is manual labor. The same two guys who mow the lawns, weed the flower beds, clip the hedges, and dig the graves at Parklawn also burn the bodies. They wear work boots and hats emblazoned with beer company logos. They seemed to be agreeable fellows, but they lacked that soothing, avuncular, funeral-parlor mien one grows used to in the days surrounding a death. Briskly, they rolled the trolley over to the oven door.

"This is going to take a while," one of them warned me. "We're talking four, five hours—young guy like this here."

"Big fella too," the other one agreed. "Could take five and a half."

"They'll either use propane or natural gas for the cremation," Mr. Moss was telling my mother, in his soothing, gentle voice.

"Really?" Billy said. He elbowed me in the ribs. "Well, if you ask me, Drew would have wanted it to be natural gas."

Drew's father snorted. "*Natural gas?* I'm telling you, that's going to be the hottest goddamn fire this place has ever seen!"

Mr. Moss, apparently under the impression that this

(like the composition of the coffin) was an environmental issue, went off to find the director of the crematory. He came back to assure us that natural gas would indeed be used.

"An older person you can sometimes do in three. Their bones break down faster," one of the workers was saying. "Even in four hours, the big bones—your pelvises, your femurs—they don't burn. They pretty much stay as is."

"Then what?" my mother asked, clearly picturing someone trying to jam a half-burned pelvis into an urn. "What do you do with the big bits?"

"We grind them up in that grinder," the guy said, pointing to what looked like an oversized Waring blender. "And then put 'em back in with the ashes. It works really well," he assured us, mistaking our bemusement for skepticism. "Grinds everything up nice."

Billy wandered over and casually inspected the grinder, just to make sure that there wasn't too much of anyone else in there who might get blended in with Drew.

Somewhat too quickly, one of the workers opened the big stainless steel doors to reveal a smaller cast-iron door. It looked like the door of a woodstove or the doors one sees in pictures of the crematories at Auschwitz, though we tried not to notice the resemblance. He opened it, and behind it was a smallish brick-lined oven not a whole lot larger than Drew's coffin. The workers pushed the box into the oven.

"So long, my buddy," Drew's dad said.

"I will see you in my dreams," I said.

If you ask the children what they remember about the first six months after their father's death, they will probably say something like, We cried a lot.

We discovered that you can carry on a conversation and cry at the same time. You can cry while vacuuming the living room. You can cry while ordering pizza over the telephone, although the conversation is longer and more confused than it otherwise would be and you sometimes get a topping you dislike.

You can weep while coloring. Sitting on my lap, Woolie got tired of coloring sky and asked for help, so I scribbled away with the blue Crayola. I still have that drawing. The sky has wet splotches where Mommy's tears fell. My children grew accustomed to having a mother who leaked tears, although it bothered them when I actually sobbed.

Peter discovered that it is possible to weep while emptying rainwater from garbage cans. Zach wept while taking out the compost, while folding pillowcases, even while riding a bicycle, though he advises against doing that on a busy street.

You can weep while putting a CD in a CD player. But when it comes to music and mourning, stick to instrumentals. Songs with words are booby traps. You think you're okay, then some sweet-voiced crooner starts singing of loss in a minor key, and you aren't just leaking water from your eyes, you are down on the floor and grief is a splintery thing the size of a telephone pole, shoving its way through your chest. My advice: listen to classical music, preferably baroque.

Alanis Morissette, bless her heart, had recently released an album called *Jagged Little Pill*, and the children and I used to listen to it over and over while we drove to and from preschool and swimming lessons and karate.

We would sing along: "I feel drunk but I'm sober . . . I'm brave but I'm chickenshit," and Woolie would shriek with delight, kicking her heels against the front of her car seat: "Again! I want the song about the chicken again!"

Alanis was safe for me to listen to because all her songs were angry. The sole stage in Elisabeth Kübler-Ross's stages of grief that I seemed to be skipping was the anger stage, because there was no one to be angry with. Drew's death was an accident. No one intended it: not the speeder he was turning to go after, not the driver of the truck, not Drew himself, God knows. So I wasn't angry. It hurt. That's all.

Eventually, we would get around to scattering Drew's ashes down by the lighthouse in Port Clyde, where a rose marble memorial bench would bear his name and dates, and the tushes of sea-gazing tourists, in perpetuity.

I would be taken care of. I would take care of my children, and we would take care of each other.

Logically enough, the children concluded that their cremated father (the one "who art in heaven"—we said that prayer a lot) was reachable via smoke. Periodically over the years, they would take their best pictures and their laboriously written notes ("DAb loVe MOOLIE") and burn them on the driveway, their grief diverted nicely into childlike pyromania.

Oh, they would grow and wax strong in spirit, and I would see their father, my *objet d'amour,* in the shape of Ellie's mouth, in the gesture of Peter's hands, in Woolie's eyes and flatulence, and in Zach's outrageous white-toothed grin. Eventually, my heart—my fragile glass heart—would again be offered to the mortal hands of another man guaranteed to break it, one way or another, since that is the lunacy and loveliness of love.

But at the end of that day—the day of Drew's cremation, the day his beautiful and beloved body was burned and ground to dust—it was not yet time to walk away.

I was still with Drew, and he was still with me, or at least the urn, my transitional love object, was with me. I held it on the lap of my pretty dress, my arms encircling it as we drove home. It was still warm.

Alanis Morissette sang on the radio.

"Make sure that when I die, you remember to have me cremated at Parklawn. Put me in the same oven they put Drew in," I said over my shoulder to my mother in the backseat. "If you're facing the ovens, it's the one on the left."

"Ooh, me too," Billy urged.

"I'll remember," Mom said.

Chapter Four

When I was nine years old, I had an encounter with the Risen Christ. Friends, let me testify.

My parents and I were driving to our house in the country late one night. I was lying on the backseat of the station wagon, half asleep. I don't know where my siblings were; their absence, in fact, might account for the sense of abundance and well-being I felt, as the wheels hummed beneath my head and the telephone wires looped rhythmically, endlessly past the windows. And then . . . there He was. Jesus Christ.

He was instantly recognizable. He looked like all His portraits in the *Random House Children's Bible*—serene, Caucasian, stretching His enormous hands toward me out of a queer, blue light. He did not travel with me, the way the moon did, but slid past the window with the trees and the telephone poles. In seconds, He was gone.

I pondered this in my heart all weekend, and by Sunday I was a believer. Sunday was the day my parents returned to the city, and, sitting up in the back of the station wagon in the clear and rational light of day, I saw Jesus again. Only this time I saw that He was a large fiberglass statue surrounded by blue spotlights and presiding over the landscaped grounds of the Mountain Rest Memorial Garden. How embarrassing.

Luckily, I hadn't told anyone about my vision. In my secular family, an announcement that I had seen Jesus would have gone over like a lead balloon. And the Jesus business went out of my head soon enough anyway, replaced by more pressing nine-year-old matters, like learning long division and making parachutes for earthworms. I didn't give Jesus another thought until my friend Pamela was born again.

That was in the seventh grade. By that time, my family had moved to the country, to a little town surrounded by farms and populated by people for whom parturition and football were the standard metaphors for grace. Everyone in Pamela's family had been born again, and her older brother had actually been born again and again and again, as he kept retreating into the womb of alcoholism to gestate a bit more before reemerging into the light.

Because she was my friend, Pamela naturally hoped that I, too, would be born again. She liked me, after all, and it bothered her that I was going to spend eternity being stir-fried in the Devil's wok. Earnestly she implored me to come to Jesus and be saved.

My father was technically a Lutheran, having been christened as an infant at a little butter-colored church in Denmark, but he didn't practice any religion now. The person who borned me the first time—Mom—was at best an agnostic. From all Pam told me, Mom was definitely going to hell. That made hell into desirable postmortem real estate as far as I was concerned.

But Pam begged me to go to a prayer meeting with her, and out of curiosity as well as friendship I agreed. On the way there, Pamela's father sang along to WMAR, Christian Country Radio—"where the spirit rides the airwaves."—"Drop-kick me Jesus through the goalposts of life."

Oy vey, I thought.

Pam's born-again church was huge. It was easily ten times the size of the little island chapel my occasionally Episcopalian grandmother attended when she took up residence in Maine in July and August. And it was thronged with people, including hundreds of adolescents wearing T-shirts with messages like PREPARED FOR RAPTURE and TEENS FOR CHRIST.

As Pamela, her family, and I entered the crush and were pressed through the big glass doors, I experienced a sudden and acute anxiety. What if . . . What if I became born again? That is, what if being born again was something that could happen like a bolt from the blue, against your will, against your upbringing? And what if, once it happened, short of dissolving into alcoholism, you couldn't get un–born again? What if I ended up going to heaven with all these teens for Christ, instead of to hell with Mom where I belonged?

The minister was younger than I expected and was wearing blue jeans. He howled the Good News into his microphone like Elvis singing "Hound Dog." The sound system boomed disco hymns, and the teens for Christ waved their arms in the air and boogied. Pam boogied. I was too tense to boogie.

"Open your heart!" the minister implored. "Open your heart to Jesus, and let him come in!"

No! I refuse! I am the child of lapsed Lutherans, seasonal Episcopalians, and near atheists. My people do not wave in the direction of heaven. We do not boogie with God!

"Now I'm asking y'all to turn . . . Turn . . ."

I won't. I will not.

". . . Turn to the person right there next to you, right there, your very own brother or sister in Christ, and I want you to offer unto that person a big ol' Christian embrace. Can you do that for me now?"

Everyone in the congregation began hugging.

I turned to Pamela, but Pamela was already offering a Christian embrace to the person on her right, so I turned the other way. My neighbor was a middle-aged man holding out his hairy hands in my direction.

"Jesus *loves* you, honey!" he declared, and mashed me firmly against his torso. After a few long moments, I began to realize that the embrace this man, my brother in Christ, had offered unto me had a distinctly—how shall I put this?— *secular* feel.

However disagreeable it was to get groped at the born-again church, the experience was bracing. I returned to the bosom of my family a skeptic, scornful and relieved.

CHAPTER FIVE

I spent my nineteenth year volunteering in a hospital. I wore a pink dress with a candy-striped apron, and I worked with very old people who thought I looked pretty dressed that way.

My job was to hang around and talk with them if they were lonely, to brush their dentures, and to rub their backs with Keri lotion. (To this day, the smell of Keri lotion brings back the sounds and sights of the geriatric ward.) What I thought I was doing was preparing for a career in medicine. I took premed courses at Georgetown University my first year there and thought I'd end up as an immunologist.

If I look back on my work in the geriatric ward, however, it's clear that I was drawn not so much to the science of cure, or even to the techniques of care, but to a communion with my patients that I as yet had no language to express.

Sometimes I read from the Bible, if such was requested of me. A 103-year-old lady, Annie Payne, just loved to hear the

Good Book read out loud. And I mean *loud*. I have fond memories of the senior staff physician and his coterie of medical students waiting in Annie's doorway during Grand Rounds, while I finished bellowing the Twenty-fourth Psalm at the top of my lungs: "The earth is the Lord's and the fullness thereof . . ."

Annie didn't particularly care what part of the Bible I read, and as I didn't know my way around it in those days, I would just let it fall open and start reading at random. There is some bizarre stuff in that book, let me tell you. And there I'd be, hollering about how Joshua kills every man, woman, and child at Jericho, after the walls came tumbling down; or how Jeremiah thinks the Israelites are whores; or how a peevish psalmist wants God to smite somebody's hip and thigh or smash an infant's head against a rock. And there Annie Payne would be, all bent up in her bed, saying, "Oh, it's so true. It's so true!"

I found some good stories and some decent poetry in the Bible, but I didn't find God. I just loved being with Annie Payne.

But not all the time. Sometimes I would just go through the motions, bellowing Isaiah, brushing her dentures, helping her onto the bedpan and off again, and I'd be thinking about something else entirely—usually guys.

At other times, though, I would be doing one or another of these tasks, and all the specifics that separated me from Annie—age, race, class, state of health, who needed care and who provided it—would fall away, and we would just be there alive together. And that would be a moment vibrating, in some sweet and startling way, with all the electric potential of love. And then it would be gone, as evanescent and indescribable as a dream.

Eventually, and peacefully, Annie Payne was gathered to her ancestors. By then it had become clear that I lacked the stomach and the math skills for medical school. So I gave up the candy-striped apron and working in the hospital so I'd have more time for study and for being wooed by Drew. Because I did not belong to a church and would not have described myself as religious, at that time ministry did not present itself as a career possibility.

"By my works I shall show you my faith," says the Letter of James (2:18), but Annie's Bible never happened to fall open at that page.

January 1998. I heard Drew's voice in the other room.

"Do you need help?" he asked me. "I'll be right there."

His voice was louder, brighter than life. And for a few seconds, this did not strike me as remarkable, even though it had been well over a year since Drew died.

The kids were watching a videotape, a family movie shot with a camera Drew had borrowed from the state police drug unit some years back. It was the middle of the week, the middle of the day, but I didn't have the heart to remind them of the rule. Although I was trying to keep up with rules, all the rules Drew and I made together, earnest parents we: whole wheat, brown rice, no sugar, no television, no videos except on weekends, and even then only at night. It was the middle of the week, the middle of the day. The children were watching a movie that contained their father's voice. Even if I could have removed myself from bed (because I was still in bed, or rather back in bed, having not had the heart for the day at all, really), I could not make them turn off that voice.

"Do you need help?" I heard him ask.

I would have to be up by six the next morning to get to my first seminary class in Bangor by eight. The children would have to watch the clock on the microwave and leave for school when it said 7:35—I was worried about this. Zach assured me that he could lead the exodus, but he was only eleven.

Yes! I need help! I can't do this. And I want you here, your body pressed to mine in a bed that reeks of us. (Oh, that half-remembered smell, fertile as loam: if someone opened a packet of seeds and scattered them across our bodies, they would sprout.) *Drew, I'm afraid I won't be able to make a life without you.*

"I'll be right there," his voice assured me.

In the morning, bright and early, Woolie awakened me by biting my arm hard.

"Ow!" I shrieked, and Woolie sat up on what was now her side of the bed, startled.

"Oh, I'm sorry, Mama," she said, with sleepy sincerity. "I dreamed you were Peter."

I made it to my first class at seminary right on time.

When it was clear that I was determined to enter the ministry, my younger brother sent me a gallant congratulatory e-mail, full of concerned fraternal inquiries about minister's pay scales and employment benefits. It wasn't until the very end of the note that he asked the pressing question: "Dear Kate," he wrote, "you don't really believe in God, do you?"

E-mail is a medium made for misunderstandings. I assumed my brother was being a jerk. Had he been in the room rather than on the other side of the continent, his facial expression or the angle of his head might have transformed the meaning of his words from supercilious challenge to gentle teasing, or even to earnest yearning inquiry, but my Inbox could admit nothing but words.

On the other hand, this is my brother we're talking about. We're a family of snotty know-it-alls. We don't do "earnest yearning inquiry." So I'm sure I know exactly what he was thinking as he wrote those words: *My sister's gone over to the Dark Side. How am I going to explain this to my friends?*

So he taps out a few innocuous questions about health insurance and retirement packages, just to lower my guard. We are siblings after all: the shields go up as soon as the handwriting on the envelope, or the screen name in the

Inbox, is recognized. But as soon as I relax, there's the kicker: "You don't really believe . . ."

Dear Kate, he wanted to say. *Now that your husband has died, now that our father has passed on, I am the eldest male in your life. It falls to me to talk you out of this religion thing before you end up in the harem of some Kool-Aid-guzzling apocalyptic.*

It was one thing when you and Drew were attending church. That's like joining a bowling league or something. A little lowbrow, but the entertainment options up there among the double-wides in the Frozen North are limited. It was difficult enough to imagine you in a pew every Sunday. You were such a rotten kid!

Sure, I remember the time, circa 1971, when you invented a religion. I don't know what your doctrines were, but you made all the neighborhood kids drape themselves in bed sheets. We sang "Point Me in the Direction of Albuquerque," and I banged on the spaghetti pot with a wooden spoon. And now that I think of it, whenever we all got together to play wedding, you always wanted to officiate.

None of this struck me as significant until recently, when I came across an article about a neurological disorder called temporal lobe epilepsy. This disorder induces, among other symptoms, overwhelming, oceanic sensations of religious awe. Maybe—and don't take this the wrong way; I offer this with purest brotherly concern—maybe you have this disorder? Present since birth, it has expressed itself under the stress of being recently widowed. But don't panic! I'm sure this condition could be cured or controlled with medication. Visit your doctor soon, please, before you end up as pope. LOL.

Few knew that Drew had been actively considering a second career as an ordained Unitarian Universalist minister. Within a year of his death, I had matriculated at the Bangor Theological Seminary. I planned to be ordained and to serve Drew's brothers- and sisters-in-arms as a law enforcement chaplain.

Mine is a sweet little story, one that has what my journalist-father used to call a "great hook." When local newspapers run human-interest pieces about me, the story they invariably tell is the humanly interesting tale of a plucky widow taking up her husband's standard and bravely soldiering on. It is the same tale I would tell on those not-infrequent occasions when seminary professors would inquire about the nature and occasion of their students' "callings."

Many of my fellow students were coming to the ministry from lives marked by recent trauma or loss. They were also—and this was a relief—mostly middle-aged, second-career students. Like me, they had manifold responsibilities and commitments. We proceeded so slowly and in such small batches through the course of study that I once suggested to a startled dean that we call the seminary an ovulary.

The Tale of the Plucky Widow was at least somewhat true, and I told it with conviction. So my less romantic advisers worried that, like a Hindu widow immolating herself on her husband's funeral pyre, I was sacrificing my living self for the departed dead. Or, less dramatically, that I was merely rearranging stones on the grave instead of getting on with my new, Drewless life.

I do not dismiss the notion that I might have been trying to keep Drew with me by doing his work. Drew and I, as a long-partnered pair, did in some sense become intertwined elements of one richer whole. Together we made a family; together we chose our church and entered into the life of our faith community; and together we made our commitments to it.

When we discussed his plan for the future, therefore, we had actually been discussing *our* plan. And I would cheerfully admit mine to be a hand-me-down calling—I, a mere understudy for this God Gig—were it not for an almost guilty self-awareness: I studied for the ministry because I wanted to be a minister. Blame it on the configurations of my temporal lobes. Blame it on the Blue Jesus of the Highway. But I wanted to do the work.

But are you really going to make a career out of defending those ancient fairy tales about the creator of the universe? my brother wanted to ask me. *God as an old granddad, with a jeweler's loupe screwed into one eye, adjusting the antennae on a parasitic wasp while the sun sets on the fifth day?*

And then, on the sixth day, with dwindling energy and some spare clay, God makes this repulsive, bipedal creature with a head like a melon, naked skin, and smelly patches of hair. I can just hear Mrs. God snickering. "What is that supposed to be, darlin', a self-portrait?"

And God, getting all offended and sort of defiant, the way we men do, huffed life into us, just to show her.

You know, I took a required course called "The Bible as Literature" in college. So I do know something of your man, Jesus. A Middle Eastern guy with a strange gleam in his eye. He'd never make it through airport security without a strip search, but nice enough once you get to know him. Still, he doesn't have the personality of a deity. WWJD, Kate-o: I can imagine this character bothering to do a lot of things, but making a Venus-sized planet out of incandescent gases is not one of them. LOL.

New acquaintances, on discovering what line of work I'm in, will generally explain a lack of interest in church by announcing, "I'm spiritual, but I'm not really religious."

Trooper Drew Griffith was spiritual, which is to say that he had experiences of the numinous that were both spontaneous and deliberately cultivated. He engaged in a regular, deliberate practice within a chosen faith community in order to nurture his own spiritual development and to translate it into useful, loving social action. Drew was religious.

"I'm religious, but I'm not really spiritual," I told my Christian Doctrine professor. Even that probably put too fine a point on it. Mine, in reality, was a pretty plain and practical calling: I needed to do something.

I highly recommend divinity school for anyone recently bereaved. With rare exceptions, your classmates will be unbelievably nice, sensitive people. They are eager to practice their pastoral skills, so if, for example, you are suddenly moved to fits of weeping during class, your colleagues will happily abandon a discussion of Hebrew phonemes or the doctrine of predestination to put their arms around you, murmur soothing prayers in your ears, dry your tears, and bring you a glass of water. And they will accept, at least for the time being, a simple answer to the profound and complex question, why are you here?

I'm here because Drew isn't.

Of course seminaries are filled with survivors of trauma, my brother wanted to say. *Posttraumatic stress disorder is probably the least of their worries, there in the admissions office. I imagine epidemic schizophrenia, hallucinations, and a fondness for mind-altering substances, not to mention this temporal lobe epilepsy I've been reading about, are far more common. I should think being a few sandwiches short of a picnic, neurologically speaking, is the sine qua non of religious life. Before you plunk down your seminary tuition, Kate, maybe you ought to consider whether your main man Jesus himself had temporal lobe epilepsy. They didn't have magnetic resonance imaging and psychotropic meds back then, so he died on a cross in Palestine.*

Ever since, Jesus's followers have been trying to convince themselves that somehow, through his death, something in the fundamental nature of reality changed. But Kate, my poor, neurologically impaired sister, listen to me: nothing changed.

It is as inescapable as Auschwitz, Ground Zero, and Darfur. Jesus uttered the words that were his last, "My God, My

God . . ." and the earth seized and shuddered, but it did not break. The last day did not come and will not come, and death retains its sting. The unredeemed world continues exactly as before. Innocence is crushed in ordinary cruelty, the venom of asps remains beneath our lips, our paths wind through ruin and misery, and the way of peace we have not learned.

No matter what the Bible says, you should believe me, my sister. I'm not just a Braestrup, I'm a lawyer.

Perhaps forty minutes after I had heard the news of Drew's death, I was sitting in the living room with my friend Monica when the doorbell rang. The sergeant was on the telephone, so Monica sprang to answer it.

A young man stood on the front steps, clad in a spiffy dark suit, his hair neatly combed, exuding a scent of soap and virtue. Holding out a pamphlet, he beamed at Monica. "Have you heard the Good News?"

For a long second, Monica glared at him, not sure whether to punch him or laugh hysterically. She compromised by slamming the door.

A few minutes later, the doorbell rang again. This time, I answered it. It was my neighbor, an elderly woman I had exchanged no more than a dozen words with in the ten years I'd lived in Thomaston. She had pot holders on her hands, which held a pan of brownies still hot from the oven, and tears were rolling down her cheeks. "I just heard," she said.

That pan of brownies was, it later turned out, the leading edge of a tsunami of food that came to my children and me, a wave that did not recede for many months after Drew's death. I didn't know that my family and I would be fed three meals a day for weeks and weeks. I did not anticipate that neighborhood men would come to drywall the playroom, build bookshelves, mow the lawn, get the oil changed in my car. I did not know that my house would be cleaned and the laundry done, that I would have embraces and listening ears, that I would not be abandoned to do the labor of mourning alone. All I knew was that my neighbor was standing on the front stoop with her brownies and her tears: she *was* the Good News.

I could see my brother striking the keys sharply:

And if your God existed, I would tear out his all-seeing eyes for what he has done to you and to your children.

But there is no God. Gaze up at night and you will stare into a vast, black universe, a place in which our neurons spark to no effect, like signal flares no one will ever see.

"I wish I could do more," my neighbor said, and all I could think as I gazed at her, shining before me in the electric air, was *What more need there be on earth than this? Than you?*

"Why are you here?" my seminary professors asked me.

"You don't really believe in God, do you?" My brother wrote.

Dear professors, dear brother. It is possible that God is the way Annie Payne used to lean her old head against my shoulder, trusting me as I held her on the bedpan; Drew's arms holding me in our fertile scent; Ron Dunham walking out of the woods hand in hand with a child lost, then found. It is possible that God is my neighbor with her pan of brownies standing on my doorstep. It is entirely possible, that is, that the God I serve and worship with all my body, all my mind, all my soul, and all my spirit is love (1 John 4:8). It's enough. It's all the God I need.

Well, my brother sighed into cyberspace. *I shall have to comfort myself with the thought that you could be doing something even stupider with your life than ministry. You could be performing liposuction or writing political speeches or manufacturing face cream from human placentas. LOL.*

Then my brother shrugged, smirked, deleted everything but the salutation, the practicalities, and the question—"You don't really believe in God, do you?"—and hit Send.

CHAPTER SIX

I'm here because Drew isn't," I told my professor on the first day of seminary. It wasn't true. That evening, I was walking across the courtyard toward the library and the parking lot beyond, and I saw Drew standing in the library doorway, more clearly than if he had actually been there. He was wearing his bright red winter jacket. He smiled at me. *He is here,* I thought. *I carry him.*

Drew was interested in spirituality for its own sake—he was about halfway through Sogyal Rinpoche's *The Tibetan Book of Living and Dying* when he died, for instance—and would have had a fine time exploring all the spiritual systems seminary would have laid out before him. He would have enjoyed the one called "Christian Systematic Theology," and the poor professor would have found being Drew's guide infinitely preferable to being mine.

I have neither the inclination nor the talent for systematic theology. In the arguments between and among competing theories, I find sport, intellectual interest, moments of satisfaction, but no grace. Eventually, I pop my claustrophobic head out of whatever spiritual cul-de-sac I've wandered into, and impatiently demand: but what should *we* do?

"Life is meaningless," Zach announced sepulchrally. He was thirteen years old, an utterly disagreeable age for all concerned. He had already picked a fight with Ellie at dinner (informing her, after devouring three helpings of her lasagna, that her cooking "sucked"). Sulking after a reprimand, he rocked backward in his chair and broke it. When supper ended, he went off to take a prolonged, if somewhat overdue, shower and used up all the hot water. Once his smelly, resentful siblings had gone to bed, Zach, radiantly clean but still miserable, flung himself onto the old leather sofa, scattering all the careful piles of books and papers about the patristic Christological debates I had assembled.

"Hey!" I protested. "I'm working here!" I retrieved a sheaf of papers labeled "Ignatius of Antioch on Docetism" and whacked him with it. He didn't budge. "Look, Zach, I really need to read these papers for school tomorrow. Maybe you still have chores to do? Aren't you in charge of cleaning the downstairs bathroom?"

Study Questions:
Did Christ suffer only in appearance, or was his suffering real? If it wasn't real, how could it be said that he was truly

human, since humans truly suffer? If Jesus's suffering was real, how could Jesus be God? Can God suffer? Can God be God without suffering?

"Seriously, Zach. I need to do some work here. There's a new can of Comet in the cupboard under the sink," I hinted delicately. Zach sighed, but did not answer. I returned to Tertullian's treatise on the Incarnation and tried to concentrate.

Another heavy sigh bubbled from between the sofa cushions. Then it wasn't a sigh; it was a sob. *Damn!*

Zach lifted a tearful face from the sofa cushions. "What's *wrong* with me, Mama?"

"Oh, honey." I abandoned Tertullian, Irenaeus, Athanasius, and Origen and gathered my son in my arms. We sat entwined among the crumpled papers. Under the reek of soap, I caught my boy's scent. "It's puberty, Zach," I told him. "Just puberty."

"I hate it!"

"Of course you do, my darling. Everyone hates puberty. It's a natural part of life, preparation for becoming a father . . ." Blah blah blah.

Zach interrupted. "I don't want to be a father!"

"Don't worry, you can't yet. At the moment your body is merely gearing up to grow armpit hair."

Zach snorted.

"Seriously! Give yourself a break, here, sweet pea. You can't produce a nice crop of armpit hair and simultaneously create meaning . . ."

My son's scrawny body, clasped against my bosom, began to shake.

"Hey, are you laughing at me?" I tickled him violently. "Huh? Huh? Laughing at me?" And he shrieked and hooted.

I felt a pang of anticipated loss, sharp enough to prickle in my eyes: it wouldn't be long before Zach would be too big to sit on my lap or be tickled out of an existential crisis.

"I hate puberty," Zach said again, once we'd calmed down.

"Me too. Of course, I was a much, much more screwed up adolescent than you could ever be," I assured him. "Ask your uncle."

"Really? Like, what did you do?"

"Omigod! I wet my pants until I was, like, fourteen. I had a terrible temper. I shoplifted. I had the wrong sort of hair for the seventies style and was hopeless with eyeliner.—Stop giggling, cupcake, I'm trying to convey important moral wisdom, here.—And for all that, you'd think I'd have armpit hair down to my elbows, wouldn't you?"

Zach, happier, went off to clean the bathroom before bed.

"For if he was incarnate by transformation and change of substance," Tertullian advised,

> Jesus would then be one substance made two, of flesh and spirit, a kind of mixture, as electrum is an amalgam of gold and silver. Thus he would come to be neither gold (i.e., spirit) nor silver (i.e., flesh), since the one element is changed by the other and a third thing is produced. Then

Jesus will not be God, since he ceases to be the Word, which was made flesh, nor will he be flesh, that is, a human being, for that which was the Word is not flesh . . .

"But what should *I* do?" I wailed.

If you prefer applied and practical theology to the more abstract and vaporous varieties, it is difficult to find a more interesting and challenging ministry than a law enforcement chaplaincy.

Law enforcement officers, like all human beings, are presented with grand questions about life's meaning and purpose. They consider the problem of evil, the suffering of innocents, the relationships between justice and mercy, power and responsibility, spirit and flesh. They ponder the impenetrable mystery of death. Cops, in short, think about the same theological issues seminary students research, discuss, argue, and write papers about, but a cop's work lends immediacy and urgency to such questions. Apart from my familiarity with and affinity for police culture, I was sure working with cops would take me right up to where the theological rubber meets the road.

Bangor Theological Seminary is too small an institution to have a program specifically geared toward training law enforcement chaplains, but the faculty members make up for this by being enthusiastic facilitators of their students' idiosyncrasies. My professors and I designed independent studies courses exploring the intersections between law enforcement and theology, police work and pastoral care. I spent most of my first seminary summer riding on patrol with police officers from different agencies: Bangor and Portland, Maine, and the Maine State Police, of course, but also Massachusetts, Rhode Island, and Maryland State Police; Boston PD; NYPD; Newport, Rhode Island; and Frederick, Maryland. I interviewed as many police chiefs and chaplains as I could. Officially my self-directed study focused on the spiritual dimensions of the use of force by police. But the conversations were wide-ranging and rich. By summer's end, I had learned more than I could have imagined about a professional community I thought I knew inside and out.

I am still in contact with many of these men and women, and I make it a practice to schedule a ride-along with a local police department whenever I'm in a new place. While the various police agencies I contacted during my training were glad to know they were helping a cop's widow become a chaplain (no one can resist the Plucky Widow Story!), most police departments have some sort of civilian ride-along program, so I wasn't doing anything that any other student or minister couldn't have done. Indeed, I encourage any and all clergy to ride along with police officers. Among other things, it is an efficient way to identify areas of spiritual and material need in the community at large.

Ironically, I did not ride along with any game wardens or conservation law enforcement officers. For one thing, I took it for granted that I would become a chaplain for Drew's old outfit, the Maine State Police. For another, like many other

Mainers who neither hunt nor fish, I had only the most rudimentary notion of what game wardens do. I did not know they had a chaplain, nor could I have articulated why they might need one. In fact, I might have asked the same question folks so often ask of me: "What does a warden service chaplain do? Bless the moose?"

Right around the time I was sending in my application to the seminary, warden service Lieutenant Mike Marshall proposed the creation of a chaplain's position within the department to serve wardens and their families, and to assist victims and families during search and rescue missions. The police chaplain is not a common or universally accepted presence, even in state and municipal agencies where the need might be more immediately obvious. The Maine State Police had installed their chaplain, Pastor Don Williams, only a year or so before.

Thus the first Maine Warden Service chaplain, a Baptist pastor named Steve Nute (e-mail tagline: "putting the FUN in Fundamentalism!"), had to break new ground. Despite having had little or no prior direct experience in law enforcement, Steve researched the protocols for law enforcement chaplaincy, responded to evidence searches and drownings, inaugurated a program for critical incident stress debriefing, and in a mere two years created crucial precedents for the chaplain's role within the warden service.

As it happened, however, Steve's primary calling was to minister to motorcycle gangs. While the wardens were tolerant of this pastoral overlap (not to mention Steve's bushy beard and black leather outfits), the gang members increasingly resented the time Steve spent with cops. So, reluctantly, Steve resigned, and the warden service began to search for his replacement.

No one is quite sure how my name came up or how I happened to be hired. The chief of the Maine Warden Service, Colonel Tom Santaguida, remembers only that Mike Marshall walked into his office with the news that a new chaplain had been found, and her name was Kate.

"And right up above the colonel's ugly old gray head, big choirs of those holy-rolling heavenly saints began to sing hallelujah, I'll tell you what," Fritz Trisdale reminisces gleefully.

Tom notified Edna, over in supply, that she needed to order a bottle-green wool uniform jacket, men's size small, with Maine Warden Service patches on the shoulders and CHAPLAIN embroidered in red across the right breast. With this, I wear black pants, black boots. I wear a black shirt with a high buttoned collar, into which I slip a boomerang-shaped piece of white vinyl, so a little wedge of it shows at my throat. This clerical shirt also announces that I am warden service chaplain, and I wear a warden service cap that has CHAPLAIN stitched in red across the back. (My friend Monica says I look like a cross between an effeminate priest and a gas station attendant.)

Requiring an outfit with more pockets for serious fieldwork, I called the supply room and requested a set of BVDs.

"BDUs?" Edna suggested gently. "It stands for 'battle dress

uniform.' BVDs are skivvies. What color do you want them in?"

"Black. To go with my cervical collar," I joked.

So now I have a set of combat-style fatigue pants and a matching rugged shirt, with all requisite insignia, and lots of useful pockets in which to stash the tools of my trade—cell phone, latex gloves, breath mints, two mini-Bibles (one Christian, one Jewish)—and plenty of Kleenex. For winter, I have a pair of serious snow pants; a heavy parka; good, thick gloves; and warm, waterproof boots. I have a scarlet blazer for ceremonial occasions and a pretty gold badge to flash at Evildoers: Stop, or I'll pray! I am the Maine Warden Service Barbie.

Monica says I'm pretty scary when the whole kit's on. "You inspire guilt on multiple levels," she says, about sin and crime, the mistress somebody's got stashed in a trailer park, and the poached deer meat in his chest freezer.

I love my uniform. Quite apart from whatever unwholesome sartorial fetish this may reflect, my uniform is so *useful*. It tells everyone at a search or accident scene who I am and what I am good for. It also signals the many ways in which I am useless, if, for example, someone needs to be subdued, arrested, or shot. You definitely don't want me looking for you if you're lost in the woods; I can barely bumble my way from the command post to the truck without getting disoriented. Lieutenant Trisdale once suggested, not entirely in jest, that perhaps "Her Holiness" should be handcuffed to a tree, lest she wander off and make more work for everyone.

In fact, if anyone needs proof that God has a sense of

humor, here it is: I am a middle-aged mother of four who primarily works with young, very fit men. My preferred habitat is a warm, well-stocked library, yet I work in the outdoors, with outdoorsmen. But the crowning irony, the one that makes family members and old friends smile in knowing disbelief, is that I, a famously loquacious person, have a job that mostly requires me to just show up, shut my mouth, and be.

When I first started my job, I thought I had to show up and be a minister. Ministerial identity was something we had talked a lot about at seminary, but there was a big difference between a theoretical understanding of what a minister is and actually being one in the flesh.

The first search I attended was an evidence search conducted by the warden service in concert with the state police. Ten years before, a local man had disappeared. Given his line of work (cocaine dealer) and the homicidal predilections of his former colleagues and clientele, it was generally assumed that he had been murdered and his body hidden somewhere in the woods near St. George Lake. The state police detectives had received new information and called for a search of the relevant ground in case a body might turn up.

Fritz Trisdale explained why this would be a good search for me to start with. There would be a "minimal corpse," if any, and family members were unlikely to be present at the scene. I would have some leisure, at least, to observe the operation.

The Maine Warden Service overhead team had arrived at

the picnic area next to the lake sometime around six in the morning. The place was already swarming with detectives, wardens, and trained volunteers with cadaver dogs by the time I got there in my bright new jacket and brand new hat. I exchanged some self-conscious "good mornings" with various wary wardens and mystified state troopers. ("Isn't that Griffith's widow? What's she doing here?") I tried hard to appear ministerial: dignified yet accessible, holy yet humane. The clerical collar pressed uncomfortably against my throat.

Inside the warden service search and rescue trailer, conversation stopped when I entered. The guy manning the radio, the one whose laughter I had choked off just by appearing, leaped to his feet.

"Here, um, Chaplain. You can sit right here if you want. Do you want some coffee?"

They pressed me into a folding chair, from which I could watch Warden Nate Robertson choreograph the search.

Warden Robertson has calm dark eyes and a hairstyle that consists mostly of cowlicks. He is the warden service expert on search and rescue, a man of manifold talent and almost preternatural calm. A map of the search scene, marked off in sections, glowed on his laptop, and every time a search team came in, he would take the data from its handheld global positioning system (GPS) unit and download it onto the map. This translated into a series of colored lines slowly scribbled across the screen, as if a child were trying to fill a large area of a drawing with a very thin magic marker. Gaps in the search would appear, and Warden Robertson would send the teams back out to cover them.

Around eleven, a call came in that initially excited everyone. A volunteer searcher thought he might have spotted the white dome of a human skull down in a gully. It turned out to be the cap of an unusually large mushroom.

"Damn," Warden Robertson said, then he shot a quick glance at my clerical collar. "Sorry, Reverend."

"Skull might not do us that much good anyway, if they shot him in the chest," another warden observed.

"If you were to find the skull, wouldn't you find the rest of the body nearby?" I inquired.

"Bears take the heads off and play with them," Robertson explained laconically. "It's like a ball for them, a plaything with a treat inside. They roll 'em around, swat 'em, and eventually break 'em open. We find heads miles away from everything else."

"Oh," I said.

"Has anyone tried the stew at the Salvation Army trailer?" a detective asked, as he entered the trailer. "It's not bad. At least it's hot."

That bears play ball with human heads was the first, though definitely not the last, riveting and disquieting fact I would learn about death and life in the Maine woods. I learned, for example, that Maine's soil is acidic, breaking down a body relatively swiftly and thereby making old disappearances harder to solve. I learned that you can make an estimate about how long a body has been in the woods by the extent to which organisms, from molds to blowflies to coyotes, have been feeding on it. I learned that some of my favorite creatures—sleek crows, for example, and those endearingly fat-assed raccoons—being scavengers, will take turns feeding on cadavers.

I had been the game warden chaplain for perhaps a year when Lieutenant Bill Allen and I were asked to give a presentation on the emotional and spiritual stresses of finding bodies to a training class for search and rescue volunteers at Unity College. The class was composed of a characteristically diverse collection of Maine citizens: dreadlocked college students, a retired pharmacist, a large number of volunteer firefighters and paramedics whose passion for community service had not yet been exhausted, and a half-dozen middle-aged dog lovers who made a hobby out of training and working with search dogs.

Bill and I arrived at the Unity campus early, during a forensic anthropologist's presentation. She was a sturdy, sixty-ish woman who clicked briskly through a selection of color slides, pausing to point out important details ("You can see here, and here, how the maggots are clustered in the gunshot wound, as well as in the eyes, nose, and mouth"). More in boredom than in disgust—he'd seen all this before—the lieutenant wandered off to find some coffee, but I stayed where I was in the back of the room. I felt obliged to learn all I could, to prepare for my still-new ministry. And besides,

I realized, if I left, I would be admitting that I wasn't as brave as that retired pharmacist.

"Now this next slide is really interesting," the forensic anthropologist announced happily.

I braced for gore, but the slide that popped up didn't look particularly interesting. It appeared to be a photograph of a very sloppily constructed bird's nest.

"Look carefully," she urged. She told us it was the root-ball of a recently unearthed maple sapling. "You see here, where the trunk of the tree emerges? Yes? Well, examine the roots. Do you see this object here? And this one on the other side . . . here?"

The class and I gazed intently at the slide. Something round was visible through the tangle of roots, but just barely, on the left of the screen, and on the right something else, something vaguely familiar in shape, was sticking out.

"Oh my God," someone realized. "It's a foot."

Years before, a woman had died, alone, in the Maine woods. Her body lay where it fell, on the bare surface of an exposed bit of granite ledge. Near the body, perhaps eight inches away, a maple seed had taken root in an unpromising cleft that held a mere handful of soil.

"It was a terrible place to grow. The maple tree could not have survived long there. So from the tree's point of view," the forensic anthropologist informed us matter-of-factly, "this body was manna from heaven. The tree extended its root system—*reached out*, really—and, well, as you can see, it took up and encompassed the feast. The remains are almost entirely skeletonized, but are unusually intact. You see the skull emerging slightly here," she pointed to the screen, "and the foot here. With the exception of some of the smaller, left hand phalanges, all the bones were found within the root-ball. Interesting, as I say," she concluded, and the next slide flashed onto the screen.

I wanted a copy of that photograph. I would frame it and put it on my wall. That was the most extraordinarily satisfactory disposition of human remains I had ever seen.

"I would love to be buried that way," I told Bill when he got back with his coffee, "surrounded by a womb of roots, my matter broken down and taken up into a living trunk and living leaves, my grief-stricken relatives invited to hear my voice whisper in the wind through new, young branches . . ."

"It does sound nice," the lieutenant allowed, spitting tobacco juice thoughtfully into his empty Styrofoam cup.

"You don't whisper, Mom," Zach said, when I told him about the maple tree. "To hear your voice in the leaves, we'd have to wait for a hurricane."

"Whatever," I said. "Smart-ass. Just bury me under a maple tree, will you? Or maybe an apple tree. Then you can eat me in apples."

"Mo-o-om!" Zach wailed. He was, after all, an adolescent. "That is so unbelievably gross!"

"It's *beautiful*," I called, to his fleeing back.

As warden service chaplain, I am on call for emergencies statewide. When I get a call or my pager goes off, I contact the various friends and relations to whom I periodically out-source my life.

"Could you pick up Woolie at ballet for me today?"

"I wonder if Ellie could get a ride home from Rockland with you tonight after her Russian lesson?"

If the kids are at school or asleep, I leave them a note: "Hey, guys! I've been called out (drowning in Harmony). Call me on my cell phone when you get home. There's left-over macaroni and cheese for supper. Please eat it. (*No* pizza!) Keep an eye on the dogs—Clover threw up earlier. I love you madly! Mom."

Then I get into my truck and key the mike on my state-issued police radio.

"Twenty-one oh seven Augusta. I'm ten eight," I say, which means, "Good morning, dispatchers! It's your very own Reverend Kate, chaplain to Maine's Finest, and I'm working!"

"Ten four, twenty-one oh seven," the dispatcher replies, disappointingly blasé.

Civilian friends listening to the police radio traffic hear a mystifying welter of voices interspersed with static: "Twenny-one seventeen 'gusta, ten eight. Ten four twennyone seven-teen. 'Gusta twennyone fordeedoo? Twennyone fordeedoo, 'gusta, g'head. Twennyone fordeedoo, ten twenny? Ahhh, 'gusta, twennyone fordeedoo, I'm on two oh four southbound by Varneys, gotany traffic? Twennyone fordeedoo, four oh three wants you to ten twennyseven at his code five . . ."

"Do they ever call your number?" Monica asked. "And how would you know if they did?"

Game wardens can be driving with their stereo tuned to Dr. Laura or yowling along with Shania Twain; they can be in the middle of a lively debate about the merits of gay marriage with their ride-along chaplain and still—out of that scratchy, low-volume river of chatter—they will pluck the sound of their own call number, key the mike, and respond.

I tend to listen more actively to the police radio than the wardens do, because I'm nosy and like to know what everyone's doing, and because it pleases me to hear a familiar voice and hold its owner, however briefly, in the prayers of my heart.

Called to an early-morning search in a godforsaken corner of the state, I listen to the crackly voices the whole way there. Then, through the trees, I spot a cluster of green trucks with the great seal of Maine emblazoned on the side, and my heart smiles.

The young man was lying on his stomach in the frosty leaves, all but invisible in his rust brown T-shirt, his fists curled under his chest, his bare toes pointed.

"Did he lose his shoes? Why would he take off his pants and jacket?" I asked Ian Cook, the sergeant in charge of the scene.

"It's a sign of hypothermia," he answered. "When you're freezing, it can feel like you're burning up. We find people completely naked in the snow sometimes."

The young man's name, Sergeant Cook told me, was Eddie Seavey. He'd left Boston University a few days earlier, telling his roommate he was going for a long hike in the Maine woods to clear his mind after the rigors of his midterm exams. The roommate told Sergeant Cook that Seavey was a reasonably experienced outdoorsman. There were no signs of mental illness, no recent losses in love or academic standing to make anyone suspect a suicide. No one was worried when he didn't return, as promised, that night: he knew what he was doing.

"He wanted to climb a mountain and meditate," Sergeant Cook said. "Some kind of spiritual thing. And he lost his way, got too cold, died."

I climbed over a half-rotted log and just beside the dead man's hip found reasonably level ground on which to kneel. Trees and the green uniformed legs of game wardens surrounded me. I prayed without words, with silence.

"Amen," the assembled wardens murmured when I stood up, wobbling slightly. Ian Cook put out a hand to steady me.

"Praying always makes me a little loopy," I explained, and he nodded seriously, as if that made sense to him.

Because the young hiker's family was in Massachusetts, the notification of the next of kin had to be done out of state, by Massachusetts police officers. There were no relatives for me to speak with, no grieving spouse to comfort, no unshaved, beer-bellied backwoods buddies asking hesitant questions about the afterlife.

I showed up, and I knelt in the leaves beside the young man's body. I prayed. The wardens bowed their heads and folded their hands over their belt buckles.

Warden Rob Greenlaw, who had made the find, had a dead bobcat in the back of his truck. I hopped up on the tailgate and sat beside him while we waited for the medical examiner to call and give Ian Cook permission to move the body. Rob took the opportunity to edify me as to the characteristics that distinguish the elusive bobcat from the still more elusive, and endangered, lynx: "Shorter legs," he told me, and pointed also to its rounded ears and densely furred paws.

I admired the bobcat's thick, cream-colored coat, touched its strange, enormous kitty feet, its needle-sharp claws. I said mournful things about a big cat's end.

"She was alive when I found her by the side of Route 3 this morning," Rob said. "I was hoping I could get her to our volunteer wild animal vet over in Winslow, but she died on me."

Sharing a PowerBar, absently stroking the dead cat's soft fur, we talked about his glimpses of lynx, his study of bears, his reluctant respect for coyotes. We discussed the possibility that mountain lions might be making a comeback in Maine, a question about which Rob was assiduously agnostic. He told me about some other searches he'd been on, and we talked about how, if you had to choose a place to die, the hiker had found a beautiful place.

"Young guy," Rob said. "Stupid, I guess, to go off that way alone."

"A mistake," I agreed.

"My wife goes to an Adventist church. I go with her when I'm not on duty. To tell you the truth, if I could choose my church, it would be the outdoors." He absentmindedly stroked the bobcat's ears with a scratched and tender hand. "So I can understand what this guy was thinking, a little bit."

I took down the names and address of Eddie Seavey's parents so I could write to them. Ian Cook took a phone call from the medical examiner. "Good to go," he announced.

The guys from the funeral home arrived. I laid my hand gently on Eddie Seavey's plastic-shrouded foot as the stretcher was inserted neatly into the back of the hearse.

Then I got back into my truck, keyed the mike, announced "Twenty-one oh seven, Augusta, I'm back in the vehicle."

"Augusta, twenty-one oh seven. Could you repeat your traffic? You were very ten one." The dispatcher couldn't understand me. Whoops. That's why: I was speaking into the wrong side of the microphone.

Later in the week, I got a phone call from Sergeant Cook. "You know, we were glad to have you there at the Seavey search," he said. "You were a big help, to Robby especially."

"Really?" I said, racking my brain for what helpful thing I might have said or done.

"Yeah. He told me you guys talked after the search, and you made him feel a lot better."

"I'm glad to hear it," I said and hung up, mystified.

CHAPTER SEVEN

Drew was considered an unusual specimen of state trooper because he had an earring, wrote poetry, and ate whole grains.

Cops in general are not known for eccentricity. The standard law enforcement process of selection, hiring, and training tends to both find and produce a middle-class, middlebrow, leaning-toward-conservative normality. By cop standards, therefore, game wardens are a little unusual too.

Native Americans in a Canadian reservation nicknamed their local police force "the men with no legs," because officers were so seldom seen outside their vehicles. American police work is clearly a combustion-engine-driven occupation. But unlike other law enforcement officers, game wardens have legs and know how to use them. They also have, as envious deputies and troopers point out, lots of "toys": canoes, motorboats, airboats, ATVs, airplanes, snowmobiles, crampons, waders, and snowshoes. A truck gets wardens and their equipment from one point of access to another, but the truck is not the primary tool for their enforcement activity, the way the cruiser is for most police officers.

Game wardens enforce fish and wildlife laws that govern where, when, and how often hunters, trappers, and fishermen can pursue what are fast becoming rare hobbies rather than ordinary parts of rural life. The Maine Department of Inland Fisheries and Wildlife employs biologists who monitor population levels for various species and attempt to determine sustainable levels of harvest. Poachers can wreak havoc on deer populations—some years Washington County's deer have been nearly wiped out, for example—and deer can wreak havoc on the ecosystem in areas where hunting is unpopular.

Unchecked, deer transform exurban vegetable gardens and zinnia beds, as well as the vegetation other mammals and birds depend on, into abundant fat stores, and then, rapidly, into overabundant deer. Sentimental supplemental feedings of hay and corn by well-meaning nature lovers doesn't help.

A percentage of Mainers—most, though not all, transplants "from away"—think hunting deer and other animals is dangerous, cruel, and disrespectful. Hunting certainly poses hazards, and the warden service does have to search for hunters who get themselves lost in the woods. But people who hunt are generally capable of looking after themselves until help arrives, unlike those who pursue what Lieutenant Trisdale once referred to as "nonconsumptive outdoor recreation" (I pictured pink-cheeked birdwatchers and pale hunters coughing blood into their blaze orange mittens).

Of course, wardens regularly respond to and investigate hunting accidents. A number of these turn out to be not particularly well-disguised suicides, but others sometimes involve the careless use of firearms by inexperienced, irresponsible, or drunken hunters. There is no way to excuse the inexcusable.

Statistically speaking, deer hunting is not nearly as dangerous to human life and limb as is processing cows into hamburger. And deer represent a relatively cruelty-free source of organic meat. Totally free-range right up until the moment of death, deer can be deer: wild; free; browsing spring grass, tree buds, and lettuce shoots; fighting other deer for mates; enjoying the all-natural thrill of being chased by coyotes and stray dogs. Then, one day, when a deer is wandering along, thinking deer thoughts, *bang!*

"Not such a bad way to go," a warden ruminated once, but then, he was a hunter. And besides, at the time he was comparing the death of a deer to his brother's prolonged, excruciating struggle with terminal cancer—perhaps that was unfair.

Still, even if a hunter botches the job and a deer suffers before it dies, that suffering does not begin to compare with the hideous misery of the average Hereford heifer, born for the stockyard, the slaughterhouse, and the sesame seed bun. This can be difficult to convey to people whose meat comes packaged in Styrofoam and Saran Wrap, but to kill and butcher what you eat can encourage a true understanding of and respect for animals. After all, Native Americans managed to be both respectful and enthusiastic carnivores. And how many small-scale farmers tenderly scratch the backs of the hogs they will one day consume as bacon?

"Throw your nets on the right side," Jesus advised his fishermen friends. How many fish flopped and gasped their last in their Christ-blessed nets that day? So many, if you're interested, that "they were not able to haul the nets in" (John 21:6). Siddhārtha Gautama (the Buddha) died after eating a bad bit of pork; I wonder if he had been introduced to the pig?

Some hunters I have encountered do fit the stereotype of the tobacco-chewing, beer-swilling, wife-beating redneck who will shoot carelessly at anything that moves. The wardens themselves tell stories of fishermen who "cast their nets on the right side," haul in more than they can use or the waterway can spare, and think nothing of the damage they are causing when they don't throw most of the catch back. But the hunters and fishermen I know best—the game wardens who hunt and fish—are intimately and affectionately involved with the natural world. It should be mentioned here that a Maine game warden's idea of homey decor involves plenty of taxidermy, which I suppose might indicate either disrespect or aesthetic appreciation. Still, the warden works in the Maine woods, protects the denizens of the Maine woods, eats from the Maine woods, and would just as soon die in the Maine woods, given the usual alternatives—the highway, the hospital, the nursing home. Not surprisingly, game wardens tend to be well informed when it comes to Maine's natural history.

Ian Cook took me out for a ride around his district on a perfect, Maine autumn day. The sky was a rich cerulean. Big blueberry burners, squirting flame, crawled back and forth along the contours of the barrens, slowly painting long, ashy black stripes across the crimson hills. The maples crowding the edges of old logging trails formed archways of saffron and gold. It was, Ian agreed, a fine, fine day to be a game warden.

Ian lives and patrols in Washington County, which Mainers know to be the true Downeast. As we drove along, he took detours to show me vistas that, however familiar, still struck him as particularly gorgeous. And with unnerving suddenness he kept pulling the truck onto the verge to point out creatures I would never have spotted on my own: a long-beaked woodcock that glared at us with high-set, disapproving eyes from under a bayberry bush, and a lithe black mink hunting grasshoppers in a roadside patch of high gold grass. At each revelation, Ian's delighted blue eyes found mine to see whether I shared his wonder at these creatures.

Ian is a game warden and a hunter. He also moonlights as a shepherd. Before we concluded our tour of his district, he took me to see his sheep grazing in meadows overlooking the sea. In summer, he transports them out to the islands to fatten languorously, far from the mainland's coyotes and dogs.

"This group, I just brought in from Matinic," he said. "See that one there?" He was pointing to a fat young lamb.

"That's Walter. His mother rejected him at birth, so my daughters bottle-fed him all summer. He slept in a cardboard box by the woodstove until just a few weeks ago. He looks fine, doesn't he? Walter? Hey, Walt. C'mere."

Walter looked up and trotted briskly over to us, baaing hopefully for a treat. Ian reached through the wire fence to rub the lamb's snoot. "Nice fat fella you are, Walter, hey? Good boy. What a beauty you are!"

Ian's strong fingers wiggled down through Walter's thick wool and scratched the happy lamb around his neck and jaw. Walter's eyelids drooped; he was overcome with bliss.

Before Christmas, the family would eat Walter. Walter would taste just fine.

Back at his house, Ian told me, "I pinched two clergymen night hunting right there in that backfield last summer." He had already played the English fiddle, and served me a cup of Earl Grey tea out of a delicate china cup. "They'd just finished up one of those pew-jumping prayer services they hold, one of their revivals, and I guess they figured they'd caught their share of souls, they could afford to sin a little. Two deer, *bang bang,* one for each of them. I saw them do it, but when I confronted them, they lied. Lied to me and cussed too! Can you believe it?" He poured me some more tea. His wife, a strikingly beautiful redhead, shook her head. She was spinning fine wool on a lovely, hand-built wheel. "You want a scone?" Ian inquired, while his youngest daughter showed me the socks she'd knitted.

Ian would probably be offended if I told him that he and

his brother and sister wardens strike me as old-fashioned, though I mean it in the nicest possible sense. *Old-fashioned* may not be the right description, anyway. Maybe there have been, at all times and in all places, men and women who stand firmly rooted in a love of and engagement with the natural world on the one hand and a commitment to human service on the other. Leaving aside the question of whether such a life is virtuous, it appears to be both satisfying and enviably entertaining.

In his book *The Hidden Heart of the Cosmos,* cosmologist Brian Swimme offers the following exercise:

> Invite someone to visit you who lives at least twenty miles away and who has never visited you before. You can give verbal instructions on how to get to your abode . . . but the one rule is this: in your directions you may refer to anything but human artifice. You may refer to hills, oak trees, the constellations of the night sky, the lakes or ocean shores or caves . . . ponds, trails or prairies . . . estuaries, bluffs, woodland . . . creeks, swamps . . . and so on. (56)

No houses, no traffic lights, no streets or streetlights, no firehouses or Home Depots. Could you do it? I couldn't. And Swimme would argue this incapacity is symptomatic of an estrangement from our "local universe" that has become endemic in our time and place. Game wardens may be the exception, however.

While out on a training run, Warden Alex Hatch stopped to show me a calf moose, standing motionless among white birches, up to its hocks in a stream alongside Route 1A, close to the Canadian border.

"Such a teenager! Gangly body, disgruntled expression," I squeaked. "He looks just like my boy, Zach."

The moose, as if he'd heard, shot us a single, deeply offended glance over the hump of his shoulder before storming away downstream in a great, sloshing huff.

"Where is he going?" (I imagined the moose retreating to some woodland clearing beyond our earshot, where he could turn up Green Day really, really loud.)

"Well, that creek comes off the St. John River right back there," Alex said. "It joins up with Lagasse Brook just east of Madawaska, and ends up in Long Lake. So if he's so inclined, our moose could go pretty far. You know, Kate, if you could walk on water, you could step out right here, walk down to Long Lake, cross the lake and find the entrance to Mud Creek, keep on heading south . . ." and Alex proceeded to tick off the streams, brooks, trickles, and rivulets that crossed and recrossed his district and beyond, all the way to Bangor. The waters of northern Maine formed a pattern as real and familiar to Alex as the lines in his palm.

The St. George River flows through Thomaston and divides the peninsulas, leaving Thomaston on one side, Cushing on the other. It meets the sea in an enthusiastic tumult just past the lighthouse at Port Clyde. That is where the children,

Drew's father, sister, and I scattered Drew's ashes with our own hands—a messy business. Where, though, does the St. George begin? Which little creeks and rivulets feed it? I don't know. I also don't know at what point in its seaward journey it becomes brackish, then salt. I couldn't tell you where to dig for clams or find mussels. There are fish in the river, but I don't know what kind or how to catch them. Even if I could walk on water, would I know enough to let the St. George feed me and lead me home?

Chapter Eight

Mr. Levesque was supposed to be home by supper time. His wife knew he was planning to ride the snowmobile out to his ice fishing shack on Hobbes Lake, and though she couldn't recall what he was wearing when he left, an inventory of his wardrobe revealed that his long johns, a frayed gray-and-blue plaid flannel shirt, and his black and green snowsuit and helmet were missing. He was probably wearing his big black moon boots too, and maybe the electric socks he got for Christmas.

She told all this to the state trooper who was dispatched after the 911 call. Because he arrived first, the trooper had to ask questions that, however necessary, nonetheless added nuance and complexity to her fears: "Does he have any friends who maybe you don't know well, or wouldn't think of, where he might have gone? Any, you know, female friends who he might visit? What was his mood like lately? Any health problems you know about? Did he frequent bars? Any drug issues?"

"No no no. My Jean-Pierre does not drink. Not a drop, and no drugs either. He was out fishing for burbot, it being the season.

"He would have his fishing license on him," Mrs. Levesque said carefully to the game warden who turned up next.

"We'll worry about his fishing license after we find him, ma'am," the warden says, and smiles reassuringly at her. She hates the trooper by now, but the warden seems like a lovely man. He seems to get the picture when she says the urgent words: "My husband went out across the lake on his snowmobile, and he wasn't home by supper time."

"The wardens are wonderful," she will later say. "That state trooper wasn't any good at all, just kept saying my Jean-Pierre must be drunk with a woman in some motel room, but the warden went right off straight to look for him."

In fact, the state trooper asked the same questions that the warden would have asked if he had been the first officer to respond to the call. No one ever wants to gin up an elaborate ground search, calling in dog teams and volunteers, only to find that the missing person is safe and warm someplace and just didn't feel like calling home.

It happens. Last winter, fifteen game wardens and assorted hardy neighbors spent a long night in subzero weather, scouring snowmobile trails for a snowmobiler who, as it turned out, really was drunk in a motel room with Miss Somebody Else. Weren't we all somewhat ticked?

So an initial skepticism is standard. Even Ralph and Marian Moore, the parents of missing six-year-old Alison, had been subtly probed for evidence of perfidy, and the sheriff's deputy who first responded to the picnic area near Masquinongy Pond would have looked around with an apparently casual eye for anything that struck him as out of place or wrong.

Mr. Levesque had stopped at the Quik Mart near the boat launch for coffee and cigarettes and a couple of hand warmers, and the clerk wasn't sure but thought he headed off toward the boat launch. You could see Levesque's little corrugated-tin shack from there, shining in the low bright light of a rising moon. And sure enough, the warden found Levesque's pickup parked there, the snowmobile missing from the truck bed, a set of tracks going out across ice, now glowing silver as the moon rose higher.

The warden unloaded his snowmobile from his state-issued pickup truck. He rooted around under a pile of assorted gear in the backseat until he found the duffel with his snowsuit, helmet, thick gloves, and boots. The snowmobile roared to life, and the warden buzzed out to Levesque's ice shack. He noted several empty brandy bottles lined up neatly along the far wall behind a Lilliputian woodstove; a couple of fishing magazines; some fishing line, stiff with ice; and a paper bag containing wrappings left over from a meal of sandwiches, Cheez-Its, and powdered minidonuts. There was no evidence that any fish were caught that day, no scales or blood by the fishing hole. The warden shined his flashlight into the hole. Maybe two feet down, the black water reflected the beam back, but the water was beginning to ice over. It was hard to tell with his cold hand, but the saucer-sized top of the little stove seemed slightly warm. Depending on how much brandy Levesque had in him after his day of peace and solitude on the ice, he could have lost his way.

A quick circuit of the lake took an hour, and the warden paid particular attention to the little inlets and nooks into which Levesque might have strayed. One deep inlet, angling off to the left, perhaps a quarter mile from the boat launch, looked promising. The warden knew that a big stream, almost a river, really, entered the lake at that point, and the ice would therefore be uneven, treacherous, and thin in spots. He shined his powerful flashlight as far up the inlet as he could and thought he saw a dark patch, an opening in the water, but couldn't be sure. He called for reinforcements, did some ground searching on foot along the edges of the lake, and had the sheriff's department check the local motels and nightspots just in case. And he let Lieutenant Allen and the dive team know that they might be going under the ice in the morning.

Mrs. Levesque spent a long night trying to think of good reasons for Jean-Pierre to be absent. She called and re-called friends and hospitals. She pictured her husband cold and frightened, possibly in pain from an injury, hungry and abandoned under the cold sky. She imagined him sitting somewhere in a bar, warm and drunk, chatting up the barmaid. She imagined him murdered for his bait by another ice fisherman, kidnapped by devil worshippers, abducted by aliens. She did not sleep.

A neighbor came to sit with her for a time, which was a blessing, and her sister promised that she would start down from Montreal in the morning if Jean-Pierre hadn't turned up by then.

"Folks sometimes find their way back on their own steam," the warden told her gently. "Give a call if Jean-Pierre does come home, no matter how happy and relieved or angry you might be. Otherwise I'll be out looking for him, okay?"

Mrs. Levesque started at every creaking door, every sound of a car engine going by on the road, but Jean-Pierre did not return.

First light revealed not only an open patch of dark water in the inlet near the boat launch, but also a neat set of snowmobile tracks leading right to it.

By eight o'clock that morning, I am standing on the ice with Lieutenant Allen, in time to see Warden Don Carpenter, encased in thick neoprene, waddle to the hole where the black water steams. His dive partner, Rob Greenlaw, is already under water. The orange nylon tether that connects Rob to the surface is held loosely in another warden's gloved right hand. Warden Alex Hatch isn't suited up to dive yet; he'll go in after Don and Rob come out, if there isn't a find before then. Alex is going to maintain contact with the divers from the surface by radio. He carefully clips Don to a yellow tether.

"Let me hear your com gear," he says.

Don obediently replies, "Hello hello hello."

"You're good. Go ahead."

Don flumps down clumsily onto the ice under his load of canned air, and rolls into the water. The sleek dome of his neoprene dive hood is visible for a moment. Then he is under, his yellow tether running out through Alex's left hand.

"Can you hear 'em?" Lieutenant Allen asks, and Alex nods.

Alex says, "Keep talking to me, boys."

The scene is blindingly white—white ice, white sky, white birches on the shoreline caked with snow—and eerily quiet, unusually so for a warden service operation. Despite the cold, we do not huddle together, as it is generally unwise, even on thick ice, to concentrate more weight in one spot than is absolutely necessary. We don't chitchat, swap jokes, or engage in the usual banter, because an ice dive is dangerous. We focus, as if the divers' work requires our complete attention as well as their own. Retreating back into the hood of my dark green parka, I imagine our comrades groping slowly through the black water, thick with ice crystals. "It's like swimming through a Coffee Coolata," Alex told me once.

Because the incoming stream roils the debris in the water, the visibility, or "viz," is terrible. The divers have to feel around with their hands for a snowmobile or a body. I keep my eyes glued to Alex. He wears a headset with a microphone at his mouth, and he keeps shaking his head to one side as if to clear his ears.

"Damn," he says, after a while. "Don said something, but I don't know what it was."

Two heads pop up in the water, one after the other. Don and Rob haul themselves onto the ice and lie there, resting, while local volunteer firefighters are dispatched to ask nearby residents for buckets of hot water to thaw the communications gear.

"I found the sled," Rob announces, pawing the air in front of him to show how this was done. "It's just forward of the hole. I'll buoy it when I go back down."

"Are you okay to go down again? Want me to suit up?" Alex asks him.

"I'm okay. What's the air temp, anyway?" Rob wonders.

"Minus one or two."

"Shit."

When the hot water arrives, the divers hunch over the buckets, letting the steam thaw the microphones in their masks, which now dangle from their chest harnesses. I try to imagine the steam warming them as well. On other dives, I've found myself snuggling warden divers as if I could lend them maternal body heat, but neoprene insulates in both directions: neither touch nor steam can warm them through those suits.

Don crawls to the hole and flops back in. Rob flops in after him, bubbles rising. On shore, another diver waits, fully suited, in case Alex orders a rescue.

Diving is a relatively dangerous activity, even when a diver is in clear water looking at pretty fish on a reef in the West Indies. Here, the conditions were terrible: an uneven lake bed with plenty of dead trees and debris to snag a diver's lines, no visibility to speak of, and thirty feet or so of dark, moving water. "Plus," Lieutenant Allen explains, "you've got a lid between you and the air that's nearly a foot thick. There's only one way under the ice and only one way out." Just watching the bubbles rise made my breathing labored from sheer, empathetic claustrophobia.

A strange, whining roar erupted far up in the woods, where the little river ran back into the land. In a moment, an airboat powered by an enormous fan came flying down the iced-in riverbed, slid spectacularly sideways onto the frozen lake, and slithered to a stop about twenty feet from where I stood. The pilots, game wardens in Darth Vader helmets and glowing orange jumpsuits, waved.

"Nice landing," Lieutenant Allen growled.

Unabashed, the warden at the wheel flipped up his visor and greeted me. "Hey, Kate! How are ya?" It was Ron Dunham.

"I'm cold, thanks. You?"

"You know, when the ice breaks, we'll still float," Ron pointed out cheerily. "Want to come aboard?"

It was an irresistible invitation. I perched on the gunwale, fat as a winter robin in my layers of insulated snow gear. "I didn't know this thing could travel across ice," I said.

"Aw, yeah. She can skim right across the parking lot. When they find this guy, we're going to fly the body out the riverbed to Route 205. We could take it right down the interstate if we had plates on her."

"Really?" I squeaked, deeply impressed.

"No," Ron said. With a well-padded fist, he punched me gently in my well-padded shoulder. "Do you believe everything we tell you, Kate?"

"Just about," I admitted.

"That's why we like you," Ron said. He pointed to the opening in the ice. "Who's down?"

"Don and Robby. They've been under about ten minutes on this go. They already found the snowmobile."

"Won't be long then. The body won't have gone far."

"Even with the current?"

"The current isn't that strong," Lieutenant Allen said. "Unless it's got buoyancy for some reason, like he has some air trapped in his parka or something, the body'll go right to the bottom and stay there. The viz is the only thing that's slowing this down, I should think."

Alex Hatch suddenly straightened and held up his hand for silence. Then he turned his head, grinning.

"They're coming up," he said, relief in his voice. "Don has him."

Mr. Levesque's body is a stiff, black and lime green shape on the ice. His helmet, strangely shiny and new looking, rests next to his feet, one of which is still encased in a moon boot. The other is wearing a wet white sock, and I have the irrational desire to pull the boot back on it, lest his foot get cold.

The divers are off, making a waddling beeline for the dive trailer, where a thermos of scalding soup awaits. A big blower heater will blast them back to life.

"Bring him over here, boys, where the ice is thicker," Lieutenant Allen tells the remaining wardens. "We'll let Chaplain Katie grease the skids for this guy"—he makes a vague cross with his mittened hand and gazes heavenward by way of illustration—"and then we'll bag him."

I kneel on the ice near the dead man's head. His flesh is yellowish white. His wet hat still smells slightly but discernibly of Tide.

Beneath us lay eight to ten inches of water crystallized into solid form. A temporary, solid plane between liquid and gas supports the dead man, the wardens, and me. The snowmobile, now tethered to a floating yellow buoy, is under us, down in the mud where the hibernating turtles wait for spring and resurrection. I take off my thick glove. I make the sign of the cross on Mr. Levesque's hard, frozen forehead. I say prayers, as his wife requested.

"I am not a Catholic priest," I told her gently, stating the obvious.

"There is one God," she said. "You make the sign of the cross for him, on his head like so, if you find him dead. Jean-Pierre was raised Catholic," she told me, gripping my hand—

even if he didn't go to Mass much, even if he did drink brandy in his fishing shack, even if he did drive drunkenly across the ice and take a wrong turn. "He was a good man, a dear man. He would want his prayers," his wife told me, "and the sign of the cross on his forehead."

I am conscious of the softness and warmth of my thumb as I draw it across Jean-Pierre's skin. His eyes are closed. There's a booger in his nose hairs. "Into your gentle hands, dear Father, I commend the spirit of your child, Jean-Pierre Levesque . . ."

The wardens stand by quietly. On the shore, the volunteer firefighters, assorted onlookers, and a small contingent of very cold reporters from the local papers bow their heads. When I am finished, I say amen and they say amen, and the wardens move in with the body bag. Someone pats my back—a couple of good, friendly thumps—on the way past.

I can't meet anyone's eyes. What if I have unnaturally small pupils, bloodshot sclera, and a visible nystagmus in my gaze?

I don't mind saying prayers solely to satisfy other people's wish for prayers to be said. Indeed, that is what I invariably imagine myself to be doing as I kneel. So why, as soon as my knees touch down and my hand comes to rest on the forehead of the deceased, do I have this sense of communion? And why am I mildly disoriented, clumsy in my speech, and unsteady on my legs when I am finished?

"Mystery," my properly Christian friends would say. "It's just the mystery, Kate."

My hands are damp and muddy. Mud rode up from the bottom of the lake on the brim of Jean-Pierre's hat and moved from there to my hands. The wardens remind each other to tighten their abs and use their legs before prying the man's body from the ice, where it is already starting to stick. I wipe my hands on the thighs of my snow pants, but my hands will smell of thawing lake mud all day. They will smell of early spring when I go to tell the new widow that her Jean-Pierre has been found dead.

She will clasp my muddy hands, then seize my body. Literally hot with grief, Mrs. Levesque will sag against the front of my uniform jacket, and we will both descend to the kitchen floor. "I'm so sorry," I will say, holding her. Lieutenant Allen will be a big, solid shape at my back, his square hand resting on the kitchen counter, his head bent attentively over us. He will make low, affirmative throat sounds when I say, "I think it was very quick. I don't think he suffered. He looked very peaceful, Mrs. Levesque." The lieutenant's knee will brace me between my shoulder blades as I hold her. "I made the sign of the cross on his forehead. I said prayers for him."

Mrs. Levesque will put me to use as witness, as crutch, as Kleenex, as proxy for Jean-Pierre—a temporary substitute for all the neighbors, church folk, friends, and family members who will soon come bursting through her door to share her grief. I am a transitional love object, an *objet d'amour;*

I am Rab-Rab, Blankie, Jesus, Mama. What a strange privilege it is to be so used.

The lieutenant will muse, as we drive south together, "It's like standing right on the hinge of someone's life. You know? Right there on the hinge, while the whole world swings around, and that widow, or that mother or dad's life is suddenly completely different, permanently different. I've been a game warden for thirty-two years. I can't think how many people I've had to tell about a death, how many people have that memory of me standing there, saying those words. It's really something, to be on the hinge of so many stories."

"It is," I say. "It's really something."

Lieutenant Allen drives with his right hand. His left elbow is braced against the sill of the truck's side window, his left forefinger draped across his upper lip in a characteristic gesture. He'll be retiring soon. No more dive team call outs, no more death notifications, no more deaths—other than the personal ones we all might as well prepare ourselves to endure. His thinning white hair reveals a distinct tan line that travels around his scalp. On the back of his head, there's a tan semicircle where his warden service cap leaves room for size adjustments.

After a little while, the lieutenant sighs. He takes out his tin of tobacco and puts a pinch of it into the well-worn pouch this habit has created in his lower lip. "Sweet woman," he says thoughtfully. "A damned shame, really."

Chapter Nine

We were squatting in some uncomfortably prickly bushes near a bend in a river, watching a fisherman throw his line into the water. Binoculars screwed into his eye sockets, Warden Don Carpenter wondered in a whisper whether this guy—he knew him—had decided to get a license this time, and how many extra, illegal fish he might have already stashed in the Styrofoam cooler he was using for a creel.

I wondered how to discipline an errant twig that kept prodding me in a portion of my anatomy that I would rather not name. Then Don held up his hand for silence and passed me the binoculars.

"Look," he whispered. "Not there. *There.* Just to the left of that hemlock. See it?"

Holy moley, I thought. *What an adorable, fat little bird.* Its feathers were a mosaic of gray and dark brown, its breast patterned tidily in snowy white. It scratched at the leaf mold with large, grayish pink feet.

"What is it?" I whispered back.

"Spruce grouse. You don't see them often."

The grouse did not appear to notice us, even though we were crouched no more than thirty feet away. It scratched out a nice little patch of open dirt.

"Watch this," Don whispered.

The grouse paused, took a deep breath, then flung herself down into the dirt and commenced flopping and flailing.

"What's wrong with it?" I asked, alarmed. "Is it having a seizure?"

"She's having a bath," Don whispered.

The grouse jumped up, shaking the grains of dirt through her feathers, then repeated the procedure, taking a few moments between flopping sessions to preen and polish her white-patterned breast to an even higher sheen. Don and I quietly passed the binoculars back and forth, while I whispered intelligent remarks like, "Omigod. That is the cutest thing. Is that the *cutest thing?*" Completely charmed, I was willing to tolerate the improper advances of the viburnum bush if only the grouse would stick around and let me gaze at her. And she did. It took about twenty delightful minutes for her to complete her toilette. Then the spruce grouse, "spruced up," as it were, departed refreshed, and Warden Carpenter remembered the fisherman.

"Oh, shit," he said, and trained his binoculars on the riverbank, but the fisherman was still right there. He had popped open a beer, drank it as we watched, then chucked the empty can into the water.

"You know what? I don't like this guy," Don remarked cheerfully. "And I hope he does have some extra fish in that box, because if he doesn't, I might just pinch him for littering."

As it turned out, the fisherman did indeed have two brook trout over the limit, and he feebly tried to conceal that fact, which served only to confirm his guilt. With a jovial grin, Don wrote him a summons and made him retrieve his beer can.

"A good day," Don said, with satisfaction. From her spot in the backseat of Don's truck, his K-9, Tiki, anointed me generously with saliva. "Thanks for riding with me. You brought me luck."

Sometimes I think I live and work in a parallel universe. That is, I know that I live in a crass and boorish culture, a culture of shock jocks and road rage, "reality" television and thong underwear, corruption and consumerism, mean porn and meaner theology. I know all this. And still, the world I move through is rich and beautiful, and the people I work with, especially the wardens of Maine, are decent, discerning, and good.

Okay, so I frequently confuse game wardens with saints, only to be brought back firmly to earth by the groaning demurrals of those whom I would canonize. They will confess to the usual complement of sins, their own and one another's. Gossiping, they gleefully throw stones from what they readily admit are glass houses. They will speak of resentments, envies, fears, and an inordinate affection for alcohol, nicotine, and inappropriate sex partners. There are the occasional failures of friendship or fidelity. Too many of them chew tobacco, spitting their soupy brown saliva into coffee cups, so I always have to check before I sip. And they cuss.

Fritz Trisdale has the richest and most blasphemous vocabulary: "Sufferin' Christ, Your Holiness!" he'll say. "Could you come down here and do some of your holy rollin', Pope John Paul minister-type business? We've got another drowning. CheezusMary'n'Chosef. With one thing and another, I don't see how the jeezly Maine taxpayer can expect me to get my paperwork done."

Fritz loves to garden and to cook. He gives me tomatoes and squash in the summertime, and jars of homemade basil pesto, redolent of garlic.

"The warden service is like an Italian family," Colonel Santaguida says. "It's all about food." He's half Italian, so he knows.

Until I began working with game wardens, I had never eaten smoked brook trout, stewed moose meat, venison chili, or "skidder wheel" doughnuts, which are just like ordinary doughnuts, but enormous. (A skidder drags logs. Its partner is the feller-buncher, which sounds like an Australian insult but refers to a huge, terrifying beast that lumbers around on paper company land, snipping and gathering great bouquets of tree trunks for the skidder to haul from the forest.)

Like other law enforcement agencies, the warden service holds an annual awards banquet. It's the only banquet I know of, however, where the honorees do the cooking. I'll show up at the dining room of a fish and game club commandeered for the occasion and find Lieutenant Trisdale back in the kitchen, his green uniform shirtsleeves rolled to his elbows, white apron tied on, his glasses foggy from the steaming pots. He'll have some young wardens back there with him, rolling out biscuit dough or mashing potatoes while he adjusts the seasonings on a baked salmon.

My job at these gatherings is, as Fritz would say, "to do the Hail Marys and Heigh-ho Silvers." I give an invocation before the awards are given, and I say grace before the meal.

I did not grow up praying and therefore perhaps approach these moments with uncommon awkwardness and awe. To ask a roomful of people to "join, as you will, in a spirit of prayer" strikes me as an invitation into an almost painful intimacy.

"Join me as you will," I say and am always astonished when even the unchurched warden, the agnostic, the cynic folds his hands—gun hand and free hand, one to the other—and bows his head. Guys who invariably choose the corner table in a restaurant and sit with their backs to the wall expose the vulnerable napes of their necks on my word, out of politeness if nothing else.

The Maine Warden Service is not a church, let alone my church. The Maine Warden Service is part of the state government and an organization with employers and employees. In a civil society that rightly separates church authority from civil authority, I must tread humbly and gently when I speak to and for God here. I hope that my prayers are not experienced as an imposition or an irritant or as simply stupid. I hope those moments feel loving to the wardens, whatever it is they believe or do not believe.

I am sometimes asked whether my employment as chaplain violates the separation of church and state. After all, I am present at search scenes, the sites of drownings, the front doors of the suddenly bereaved not as a social worker or a crisis counselor. It's written right there on my shirt: I'm Reverend Braestrup. When I offer words before shared meals or warden service ceremonies, I am an obviously religious person using religious forms and language in what would otherwise be a completely secular environment. So why does the warden service need a minister?

The simple answer is they don't need me. I'm not necessary in any urgent, practical sense. For 120 of its 125 years, after all, the Maine Warden Service managed quite well without a chaplain. They could manage again, should my position be abolished. I don't make the difference between finding and not finding a body, between order and chaos, life and death. They do.

But I am told that it is helpful to have a chaplain present at a search or an accident, that by taking on the task of being with the victim's family, I free the wardens for other tasks. Perhaps more important, as a minister (as opposed to some other brand of helping professional), I serve as a symbol of a profound truth. My uniformed presence signifies a human and humane understanding on the part of the wardens and the wider community that the body in the woods or in the water is not just a practical problem, but a matter of tremendous spiritual significance for those most intimately involved. As reverend, I can express our reverence.

Still, "I am the whipped cream, not the pie," I tell the wardens, "the cream and salt, not the coffee or stew."

For me, these prayers are a luxurious indulgence, moments in which I am free to tell the game wardens that I love them: "Oh God, whose name is love and whose work is justice, I offer thanks to you for this day and for this fine and funny company," while Fritz Trisdale's biscuits bake and Nate Robertson's beans stew and Mike Marshall's smoked trout waits to be savored. In my prayer-induced stupefaction, it seems that the office of chaplain of the Maine Warden Service was generously created just to give one middle-aged woman joy.

Chapter Ten

T his is the best job in the world," Don Carpenter announced. "I love catching night hunters. I love working with Tiki here. I love being out in the woods."

"Even on a day like this?"

"Yeah, this is great!" He laughed. (Don laughs a lot.)

Under a gray November sky, the sleet found its way through the branches of the leafless trees, making every surface slick, soaking our jackets and our safety-orange winter caps. The rain managed to wick its way into the tops of my boots too. It was miserable.

"Typical tracking weather," Don said cheerfully. (He's a very cheerful guy.)

We were walking through the woods, somewhere in the vicinity of Ellsworth, following Don's tracking dog. Tiki wasn't keeping to a trail in the human sense; she was trying to locate a scent trail that might lead her, and thus her master, to the place where the body of a suicidal young woman lay.

The young woman left her baby boy at a daycare center and drove away. No one had heard from her since. Over the past couple of days, the state police dispatcher had been advising all units to be on the lookout for a blue Subaru hatchback, driver possible 10-45 (mental health issues), despondent. Finally, a couple of hunters going to the sandpits to sight in their rifles found the car. The search commenced and someone called me.

There were a lot of trees growing in close proximity here, and some of them had fallen together in big areas of deadfall that Tiki trotted through without particular effort, but that Don and I had to clamber over, under, around, and through.

Don and his wife are certified as therapeutic foster parents for severely abused and neglected kids. A little boy is the most recent addition to a family that already includes one adopted daughter, three biological children, and a lot of pets. Don described his new five-year-old son with obvious affection and his background with a sort of rueful horror. The boy had "come into care" when a New York City police officer came across him in a subway station in Brooklyn. His parents had told him to wait there while they went off to buy heroin to bring back to Maine. The child had been sitting in the subway station for four hours.

Don is a devout Baptist. He's younger than I am, with bright brown eyes and an easy, good-humored demeanor. He has that enviable quality I see in some, though not all, religious people. It's as if, no matter what the circumstances—even staggering around in wet woods looking for a corpse—he is always centered and joyful, with well-being at his core. Don's wife is a social worker, and she probably has it too, though I haven't met her yet. In addition to her day job as the mother of five, she is the supervisor of a group home for teenage boys.

"Do you two think you're doing enough for the community yet?" I ask Don. "I mean, couldn't you squeeze in a few more good works?" He just laughs. Tiki runs around sniffing and snorting and occasionally dashing over to me for a quick, friendly crotch check.

Don tells me that as a K-9 handler he had been "very lucky" for a while. "I found a whole lot of suicides and near-suicides, something like seven in a row, over maybe fifteen months."

Tiki found a man hanging in a tree on a dark night, and when Don grasped the man's foot to check for signs of life, gas burbling through the strangled larynx produced a terrible groan. "That was the one that gave me night sweats," he says. "And my wife insisted that I see someone."

"Did counseling help?"

"Oh, yes!" Don agrees cheerfully. "I wouldn't wait as long now. It helped a lot.

"Hey, Tiki, whatcha got?" Tiki is "indicating" on the water in the stream. I follow Don's eyes, and we both search the ripples for the sign or shadow of a body.

Don once found a woman, overdosed on barbiturates, passed out in a woodland stream, her core temperature reduced to ninety-four degrees. "That was a great find," Don says. "I got her just in time. She's still alive, works down at

Shaw's Supermarket. Now and then, I check on her, just to see how she's doing."

The woman we were looking for had also taken barbiturates. She had waited in the car for a little while, looking at photographs of her baby. Then she staggered off to die. She fell on the uphill side of the stream we had been walking beside. Rainwater trickling down the hill had carried her scent into the stream, where Tiki's sensitive nose had caught a whiff of it. When the call came over the radio that one of the other dog handlers had found the body, we learned it was more than a mile away from the place where Tiki had been indicating.

The body lay in a little hollow behind a rock. Her name was Betsy. She had short dark hair, and her eyes were closed as if she were sleeping on her back there in the yellow leaves.

Don, along with Wardens Hatch and Robitaille, went to the body. They began taking photographs of it in situ, in case the medical examiner or state police detectives would need them later.

Lieutenant Trisdale and I walked down the road through relentless sleet to keep a rendezvous with Betsy's brother at an intersection where the road was a little less treacherous and sloppy. We would be giving official notification right there.

As we walked, I fished my black clerical dickey out of my jacket pocket and fastened it around my neck. I tucked the edges under the lapels of my uniform coat.

"Do I look okay?" I asked Fritz, turning in the sleet to model for him.

"You look like the nuns who used to whack my knuckles with a ruler when I was in school. Listen, Reverend Mother, as long as you're here, couldn't you pray for it to stop raining?"

"I'm a Unitarian Universalist. We don't do weather," I said. The lieutenant snorted.

Fritz had Betsy's diary in his hand. The last entry was her suicide note. The diary had a bright blue cover and a bunch of little bits and pieces of paper—envelopes and whatnot—tucked in here and there, and a pen stuck into the spiral binding.

The brother's name was Dan. *Dan and Betsy, Dan and Betsy,* I repeated to myself. Remembering the names seems the least I can do in a situation like this, so I try a foolish mnemonic: Da[m]n the spot in the rainy woods where we found a bit of Betsy.

We spotted the car coming and stood waiting in the roadway. Dan drove up beside the lieutenant and stopped. He rolled down the window. Tilting slightly forward, one hand on the roof of the car, water dripping from the brim of his cap, Fritz said, "I'm sorry. We found Betsy's body. I wish there was a way to make this easier for you, but she's dead."

Dan nodded calmly. He didn't say anything.

"From the evidence we have so far, we think that after she dropped her son off at daycare, she drove out here and parked at a turnout, just down this road. She had at least forty-five sleeping pills, according to the labels on the pill bottles, and if she took all of those, it would have been enough to kill her. We found pictures of the baby in the car, and we think she probably sat there for a little while, looking at the pictures, and maybe she got some comfort from that. Then she left the car, walked up the hill, lay down in the leaves, and went to sleep."

Dan nodded. "Thank you," he said.

"This is our chaplain, Reverend Kate Braestrup."

I stepped forward, shook hands. "I'm so sorry, Dan," I said.

Dan looked up at me. His eyes caught on the collar around my neck, and you could almost hear something break in him: his whole body gave a violent shudder and folded inward on itself.

Betsy had been suffering for a long time, Dan told me. I had gotten into the car by then. I was no longer a stranger—I had held him in my arms, had his snot on my lapels—so he spoke frankly. Their parents died in a car wreck when she was seventeen, and she never seemed to quite get over that, Dan said. She had a bad spell after the baby was born, and then her husband left, and there was this really messy divorce going on, and Betsy was trying, she really was. She was in therapy and on medication, but she just couldn't seem to get herself together.

Dan asked me what was going to happen to the body. I told

him the medical examiner would need to do an autopsy in Augusta and that the funeral home would transport the body there. When the medical examiner's office released the body, the funeral home would retrieve it and would call him to make further arrangements. Yes, the funeral home had his phone number. And they were good guys; they would take good care of Betsy.

"Can the church bury her?" Dan asked me then.

It actually took him a few rephrasings to get the idea across to me, so strange and alien was it to my way of thinking: "Would a Christian church do a funeral for a suicide?"

Betsy had gone to a service at a church in Orrington the previous Sunday, Dan explained. He wasn't sure what the denomination was, but it was a new church. Anyway, the gist of the pastor's message, according to Betsy, was that suicide was the one sin that God never, ever forgave.

I pictured Betsy, her short dark hair neatly combed, alone in a pew. My chest tightened with a harsh, disorienting anger.

"So it seems like . . . I mean, that the church wouldn't . . . might not let Betsy have a funeral there, or, you know, be buried in their graveyard." Dan looked carefully at his hands in his lap, as if he were ashamed.

I hate my clerical collar, I thought.

I pictured Betsy at church with her blue diary, with her shameful, sinful despair exposed before the pastor and his pinched and stingy God.

"Um . . ." I said. And very carefully, after several deep and calming breaths: "I don't know that pastor personally. I don't know what he knows and doesn't know about severe clinical depression. Which is what your sister died of." I placed my authoritative hand on the console between our bucket seats as if it were a pulpit. "Dan," I said. "Look around." Obediently he peered through the rain-washed windshield, up the road toward the blurry outlines of half a dozen green trucks.

In lieu of righteous anger, I heard my voice take on the sure and certain cadences of preaching: "The game wardens have been walking in the rain all day, walking through the woods in the freezing rain trying to find your sister. They would have walked all day tomorrow, walked in the cold rain the rest of the week, searching for Betsy, so they could bring her home to you. And if there is one thing I am sure of—one thing I am very, *very* sure of, Dan—it is that God is not *less* kind, *less* committed, or *less* merciful than a Maine game warden."

I paused, gazing sternly into his startled eyes. *You got that, Brother Dan?*

He was staring back. He didn't say a word.

Oh dear. Maybe he thinks I'm nuts. Maybe he's trying not to make any sudden moves.

"So I want you to know today, Dan, that there is no doubt in my mind, no doubt at all about where Betsy is right now. God is holding your sister close to His tender heart. Betsy is safe, she is forgiven, she is free at last from all her pain."

"Oh," Dan breathed. "Oh."

"So . . . that's that," I finished, rather lamely. I took some more deep breaths to recover. "Would you like me to pray with you?"

"Yes I would," he said eagerly, gripping my hands. So together, there in the car, we said the Twenty-third Psalm: "Love is my shepherd; I shall not want. Love makes me lie down in green pastures; love leads me beside still waters. Love restores my soul . . . Amen, amen."

I tore a page from my notebook, borrowed Dan's pen, and wrote down the names of ministers in and around Orrington, fairly conservative pastors who knew the earth was round and knew something too of the etiology and course of acute mental illness. Dan took the paper, folded it carefully into thirds, and placed it in his wallet.

When I got back to the scene, Warden Hannah Robitaille took one look at me and went off to find a big parka for me to wear on top of my wool jacket, since I had forgotten mine, and she was sure I was going to freeze to death.

"Have you eaten anything?" she asked severely, and when I looked guilty she fetched me half a sandwich from her cooler.

While we waited for the funeral parlor guys, we rehashed the previous week's search for a missing hunter over in Kingfield. Up on the hill, Betsy's body waited in its saffron-colored bed.

At last the funeral parlor van came skidding through the mud. The funeral directors were wearing suits and ties and oxford shoes and purple surgical gloves, surreally bright against the vivid yellow leaves. They offered to climb the hill to help get the body, but the wardens told them to stay where they were. "We'll take care of it."

And I suppose I could have stayed by the van with them. I am the chaplain, after all, and a middle-aged mother of four. I pray, I give bad news, I hug, I counsel. No one expects me to lug the dead out of the woods.

But I told Betsy's brother, fiercely, that God would not abandon her. So I climbed the hill with Don and Hannah and Lieutenant Trisdale, who had held Betsy's blue diary in his gentle hand all afternoon.

I helped load Betsy into the body bag and onto the stretcher, helped with the clumsy work of buckling straps around her knees and torso. I put my hand on her cold foot, as if she could feel my touch through the body bag and be reassured. She was not ugly or sinful, just dead, and I shall carry forever the image of her peaceful, bluish face, a few yellow leaves clinging to her short dark hair. She looked like she was sleeping as Don zipped the shroud around her, sleeping as we bore her safely down the hillside under the low, gray sky.

Chapter Eleven

I gave Peter a hammer and told him to go around the house and pound the protruding nails back into the old floorboards; I thought this would prove an entertaining chore for a boy. He decided it would be even more entertaining to go down to the basement and play coal miner. I caught him whacking great lumps of concrete out of our home's foundation.

"O' faithless!" I cried out, like the God of the prophets. "I brought you into a plentiful land to eat its fruits . . . but you defiled my land and made my heritage an abomination. Be appalled, O' heavens, at this!" (Jer. 2:7)

Abject contrition does tend to provoke mercy, as sinners are only too aware. As we read in *The Book of Common Prayer,* "I have left undone those things which I ought to have done, and I have done those things which I ought not to have done." Peter said almost exactly this as we emerged from the cellar. It worked. I was merciful. The kid lived.

Over lunch at Moody's Diner the next day, I told Warden Rob Greenlaw the story of Peter playing coal miner. He laughed.

"What does Peter think of your job?"

"He thinks it's cool," I said. "And he's right."

"It's so cool that the warden service *has* a chaplain," Marian Moore said to me, just moments before the call came in that Alison, her lost child, had been found.

The first time I put on my uniform and looked in the mirror, I thought, *This is really cool.* I put my warden service ball cap on, adjusted the plastic tab on the back to account for my big fat head, and admired myself, made faces.

But then I slid the little vinyl boomerang into my collar, the sliver of white that transforms my ordinary shirt into a clerical shirt. It was a startling moment, that first look in the glass.

"CheezusMary'n'Chosef!" as Lieutenant Trisdale might say. I checked the bathroom door to make sure it was securely closed against anyone—child, friend, dog—who might come in and see me, as if I were more than naked.

The character I resemble most, I decided after some reflection, is Father Mulcahy from M*A*S*H. And why not? Like him, I am a sort of generic, ecumenical clergyperson representing the God that even atheists pray to in foxholes, an undemanding character. The comparison is apt enough. Like Father Mulcahy, I wear a Roman collar. The shocked and bereaved search my face, but the white tab at my throat draws the eye, and they fix upon it.

"Your loved one is dead," I said one winter day, and the

daughter of the snowmobile victim came close and searched my face, as if it might show that I was kidding or lying. It did not. "Oh my God! Oh my God!" she said, forcefully, as if she were angry. Then the white collar drew her eye. She took a sudden breath, "Oh my God," she said, and touched the white at my throat very gently with her fingers. Then, and only then, she sank down to the floor with me and wept.

I did not predict that reaction on my first occasion before the mirror. Instead, I predicted the flabbergasted incredulity of my friends, the sarcastic discomfiture of my then-boyfriend, the shrugs of my children who adapt well to my strangeness. But I suspected and even feared that no one who actually needed a woman of God would be fooled into thinking I was it. I have to say, though, that mourners and wardens have thus far proved to be remarkably accepting, reassuringly capable of seeing beyond me, in all my flawed particularity, to the power, mercy, and love of God and neighbor that I, by grace alone, am striving to embody.

I am one of the people who respond to a Maine game warden with love and care when something miserable or scary or painful happens to him. I am not the only person who responds, and I am not the most important one. What he really needs, in times of trouble, is the familiar, solid love of his wife, the softness of his child's cheek against his own, the smell of his kitchen, and the voice of a good buddy on the phone. If he needs spiritual counseling, the best person to do that is his own minister, if he has one.

You can get along well enough without a chaplain, but you won't thrive without family and friends. So a good chaplain should encourage wardens to establish and maintain the relationships that really make a difference. Still, a law enforcement chaplain is charged with providing pastoral care, and that includes what is known as pastoral counseling.

"The central task of pastoral counseling is not problem solving," pastor John Patton writes in *Pastoral Care in Context*, "it is hearing and remembering in relationship" (40). This sort of remembering, Patton says, can be thought of as literally *re-membering*—recalling the fact of a game warden's membership within a strong and loving community at moments when he may feel lost or alienated.

Pastoral counseling isn't the same as therapy, though it may (I hope) prove therapeutic. I am not trained or credentialed for psychotherapy. Even if I were, my relationship with the wardens is not the same as the relationship between client and therapist, with its essential nonattachment and those fifty-minute hours.

I do know enough about mental illness to have a deep respect for its powers of immiseration. If a warden has the slightest indication of a mental health problem—clinical depression, let's say, or substance abuse—I refer him to a medical professional, emphasize the blessed efficacy of such interventions, and offer myself as glad company for the journey.

I have nothing to do with promotions, hiring, or firing within the warden service. I am disengaged from the political processes that go on in state-run organizations. While some agencies have a "lieutenant chaplain" or a "major chaplain," I remain outside the rank structure. My relationship to the newest warden in the service is exactly the same as my relationship with the chief: I am his chaplain. I outrank no one.

"What are you yapping about, Holy Mother? You outrank *everyone*." Fritz Trisdale protests, when I tell him this.

"Talking to you is like talking to my big sister," Bill Allen says. Despite how old it makes me sound, I like that description: it's familial but not parental, interested but not invested. As we encounter each other at search scenes and debriefings, over bleary-eyed breakfasts at a truck stop following a long night's search, and meet at promotion ceremonies and flag-waving parades; as I preside over funerals and weddings, welcome the birth of children, and sympathize at the death of friends, the relationship between chaplain and warden grows and deepens.

"It's so cool that the warden service has a chaplain to keep us from freaking out," is what Marian Moore actually said in full.

"Ah." I smiled. "I'm not really here to keep you from freaking out. I'm here to be with you while you freak out," or grieve or laugh or suffer or sing. It is a ministry of presence. It is showing up with a loving heart. And it is really, really cool.

If my job is not problem solving, then a warden doesn't have to have a problem in order to merit the attention of his chaplain. He can just be out driving around in his truck or walking in the woods, and I can ride or walk beside him.

Warden Rob Greenlaw, for example, had no issue I was aware of. But it had been a while since I'd been out, so I called him and asked to go for a ride.

It was March, and the weather was warm enough to melt most of the snow. What remained confined itself to the areas beneath the pines that sometimes harbor snow until June. The sugar maple trees weren't quite in bud, but the tips of their branches were swollen and red. In another week, taps and buckets would appear on the ancient maples that line the stone walls along the old farm roads, and the clear, cold, sweet sap would be collected then boiled down to syrup.

Rob's district includes my town of Thomaston, so he picked me up at home. We headed down Route 1 toward Nobleboro, then turned down one of the scrawny peninsulas that dangle off the mainland into Penobscot Bay.

We were on a narrow, winding, two-lane road, chatting about this and that, when a car came screeching out of a driveway in front of us and took off, hitting sixty before Rob caught up to him, siren whooping and blue lights clacking and flashing along the front window of the truck. Maine game wardens have the same statewide jurisdiction, the same arrest powers as Maine state troopers, and they are empowered to do traffic stops. But their trucks are not equipped with radar, and Rob wasn't sure where, beneath all the heaps of fish-and-game law forms, he might have hidden his book of traffic tickets.

"He says he peeled out of his driveway because he was late for work. I asked him if he'd had a fight with his girlfriend or something," Rob told me when he came back to the truck to run a check for wants and warrants. "He said no, just late for work. He just does it that way sometimes. I told him he really oughta relax a little." Rob let him go with a verbal warning.

Farther down the road, Rob showed me a little patch of sumac and birch where someone had hauled a dead moose to use as bait for coyotes. Being in possession of a moose carcass, even assuming the guy didn't shoot the moose, is illegal, but the perpetrator would probably hold his hand over his heart and swear the moose just happened to drop dead of natural causes right at the bait site.

The moose carcass had been there for perhaps a week. It was hollowed out, and the stiff legs stuck skyward. There were a few strands of gray gut hanging from the ribs, but it was otherwise an empty shell, like a novelty canoe at some macabre water park. The skin on the knees had dried and peeled back. The joints were exposed and startlingly white. Most of the bones I've seen are cooked or weathered gray, but a fresh bone is a bright, pearly white. Above the moose carcass, the corpse of a crow dangled in a sapling.

"They hang up a dead one to scare the other crows away," Rob said. "Crows would eat the carcass before the coyotes

came, and a big crowd of crows will bring the wardens anyway. We look for them—'deputy wardens,' we call 'em."

"So this guy has the moose here to bait the coyotes in, so
he can shoot them," I said. "But why would he do that? I
mean, he won't eat the coyotes, presumably, so does he sell
the fur or something?"

Rob thought about it. "No," he said. "He'll just shoot them.
I think people have the idea that it protects the deer, but
really there's plenty of deer around here. So there's no reason for it. Coyotes are hard to shoot, which makes it more
interesting, I guess. They're smart and wary. You pretty much
have to bait them, or use hounds."

Rob wants to catch this coyote hunter. Rob knows who
he is, can identify him by the wet prints of his truck tires on
the road, and says he is "a mean guy." As with so many criminal offenders, those willing to commit one crime are generally willing to commit a raft of others, and in fact, this moose
poacher is well known to area wardens and troopers as a
domestic violence, drug, and traffic offender. A scofflaw is a
scofflaw.

Rob showed me the target's tire marks. He showed me
how to tell from the splash patterns around the puddles in
the road whether a car had driven down that way, and if so,
whether the same car had driven back out again. It had. We'd
missed him.

For some reason, the scene at the moose carcass would
keep coming back to me over the next few days. It was as if

some Druid ritual had taken place there, with the black crow hanging sideways off the tree and the white bones of the moose sticking up out of the dead grass.

"Do your children smell good?" Rob asked me at lunch, after I told him the story of Peter the Coal Miner. He and his wife had recently welcomed a second child. "My boy smells so good. I could just eat him up."

"I did eat my children when they were little," I said. "I'd pick them up off the ground and say 'Ooooh, I'm gonna eat you like an ear of corn!' I'd hold them sideways, chew along their ribs. They loved it."

"My wife does that. She munches on the baby's hands and feet, and he laughs and laughs. . . . You know, we should introduce Peter to my daughter, Brianna," Rob said. "She's about his age, and she's a ball of fire. She'd keep him in line."

Back in the truck, we drove a few miles and then stopped by the side of the road. Almost instantly, we were surrounded by a group of small, grubby children. They clustered eagerly around Rob.

"I know why you got a gun," one little boy said. "It's so if someone's bein' stupid, then you can shoot 'im."

"Don't listen to him," his sister advised. "He's a silly monkey." No more than nine, she carried on her hip a toddler in urgent need of a fresh diaper.

Another child looked up after examining the great seal of Maine on the door of Rob's truck. "Did you arrest Paul for speeding?" he inquired.

"No," said Rob. "Should I have?"

"He drives like that all the time. He's my uncle, so I know."

"Uh-huh," said Rob. "I'll arrest him next time."

The children laughed uproariously at this, and the toddler bounced on the little girl's hip and laughed too.

"Who are you?" the silly monkey asked me, pulling on my fingers.

"I'm the chaplain," I said.

"You ain't got a gun?"

"No, I don't."

"Oh," said the boy, immediately losing interest. He turned his attention back to the quiet armed man. "What kinda guns you got?"

When the children, bored at last, abandoned us, Rob and I walked a quarter mile or so into the woods to a secluded little pond. Rob showed me the telltale signs of illegal fishing: blobs of bottom detritus hanging in shrubs and drying out on shoreline stones where only a fishing line could have hauled them. The moss on the stones was bright green, the water limpid and lovely, and the day, which had started out with rain, soft and bright. I was struck by how quiet it was, by how quiet Rob was. He is a quiet man with a quiet voice and a quiet walk. He moves along the shore in big, rubber-soled boots, striding through the underbrush with no more sound than the breeze, while I blunder along behind, my breathing louder than his words.

It is Warden Greenlaw's job to get out of his truck and walk through the quiet woods as the maples swell and leaf, his job to stand and gaze across a shining lake, the scent of moss rising, birdsong in his ears. It is my job to go with him.

Chapter Twelve

So Osama bin Laden dies. He's pretty excited. After all, from his perspective he's led a righteous life and has sacrificed himself for the glory of Allah, so he's really looking forward to all the pleasures that have been promised him in the afterlife.

He arrives at the Pearly Gates, and just as he is about to scamper through, who should come toward him but George Washington. George takes one look at Osama, screams "You injured my country!" and starts hitting and kicking him.

"Ow, ow, ow!" says Osama. "What's all this?"

But before George can answer, who should appear but Dolley Madison, and she starts whacking Osama upside the head with a stick. And then George Mason, Sally Hemmings, and Robert E. Lee pile on, along with a whole bunch of other people Osama has never seen before, and they're all whacking and kicking him. Osama sticks his head up out of the pile and says, "Hey! Saint Peter! What's up with this? I was supposed to have date palms, rivers of wine, and seventy-two virgins!"

"Oh dear," says Saint Peter. "You misunderstood. It's seventy-two *Virginians*."

Hannah Robitaille told me that joke. She knows I collect jokes about religious stuff, the ones that begin "a rabbi, a pastor, and a priest walk into a bar" or "a guy dies and goes to heaven."

A boy got very drunk, walked into a pond, fell over, and drowned. The Universalist part of my denominational appellation stands for "universal salvation": everybody goes to heaven. So I can assert with the confidence of my tradition that the drowned drunk boy got there too.

His girlfriend, distraught, asked me what would happen if, as she devoutly hoped, they were one day reunited. "I mean, I could live to be eighty," she said. "He will still be seventeen. How will we get back together in heaven? How will he know who I am?"

A factual description of the afterlife is something no one living is qualified to offer. Yet, the Christian feels compelled to speak of that which is beyond words.

For anyone to get at truths that lie beyond fact, we must create myths. I don't mean that we have to tell lies. The story we tell can be wholly fictional or the story can be true. If it illustrates the organizing principles by which we understand the world and live in it, the story is a myth in the scholarly sense.

For example, how do we understand our lives? How do we understand that we have a sense of being; that we have a sense of self; that we know, create, anticipate; have relationships and ideas, memories and ambitions, and then die? And when we die, what happens to us, our soul, the self that seemed so real to us when we lived?

There are really only three possibilities:

The first is pretty simple. If the soul is contiguous with the body, or indeed, just an activity of the body, then the self dies when we die. Perhaps we can imagine elements of energy and light being released for recycling, just as the proteins, calcium, and iron of our bodies are released when ingested by bears, vultures, maggots, and hungry maple trees. But otherwise, death is death. Finis. For the most part, when Jewish scripture discusses what happens after death, this is the idea it is most apt to affirm.

The second possibility is reincarnation, in which the still-dynamic soul abandons the defunct body and resumes life in a new one. This idea is actually present in the New Testament. One of the answers given to the question "Who is Jesus?" is that Jesus is the prophet Elijah come back to life. But reincarnation may be more familiar to us from Hinduism and Buddhism. We should remind ourselves, however, that for Hindus and Buddhists, reincarnation is not really a good thing. With sufficient dedication and discipline, a seeker achieves enlightenment, and her reward is that she breaks free of the cycle of birth and rebirth, stops "coming back to life," and is at last dissolved into the All, permanently beyond suffering.

The third possibility is that a human soul has, or will someday have, a continued, conscious, individual existence in an afterlife—heaven or hell—that either does not require a body or that resurrects or re-creates the body in some invulnerable, eternal form. Eternal life is what Christians believe in. Christianity began with a Jewish prophet and retained the Jewish prophet and retained the Jewish scriptures, but the early Christians' notions of the afterlife were heavily influenced by the Greek-speaking, Hellenistic world in which they lived.

Six hundred years later, the prophet Muhammad and his followers were very much influenced by the ideas of local Christians—Christianity thrived in the Middle East in the first millennium—so Muslims developed a quite Christian, rather un-Jewish emphasis on the postmortem disposition of the believer's soul. And Muhammad, unlike Jesus, didn't fiddle around with a lot of obscure metaphors for heaven.

Muslims who take their scripture literally, therefore, will indeed expect heaven to offer date palms, rivers of wine, and seventy-two nubile young women to serve them, and here it becomes pretty clear that the Koran and the Hadith describe a heaven more or less exclusively for men, doesn't it? Perhaps I'm wrong on that. After all, I don't read Arabic, and for all I know, the word *virgin* is a gender-neutral noun. Maybe, on arrival in the afterlife, a woman can expect to be greeted by seventy-two adolescent males? But that sounds like hell to me, date palms or no date palms.

Which brings us to the heart of the problem with heaven: What would a place of perfect and perpetual bliss be like? Wouldn't it be different for seventeen-year-old boys and eighty-year-old women and different for each individual?

Funny, we have no trouble agreeing on a common vision of hell. The book of Revelation describes the misery in sulfurous detail. Medieval artists got a lot of visual mileage out of scenes of Lucifer and his minions camping out by the lake of fire, stewing thieves in a cookpot and tearing caterwauling adulterers limb from limb. By comparison, poems and paintings of heaven tend to be static, banal, and, perhaps therefore, rather uncommon.

Infinite torment was not hard to imagine for a medieval population afflicted by chronic starvation, conflict, and epidemic disease. And eternal misery is not a difficult concept for the modern with a migraine, either, or for those in mourning or suffering from arthritis, cancer, or clinical depression. So many painful experiences have real staying power.

I can't think of any pleasurable experiences in life that similarly maintain their intensity, undiminished, over time. Although a dyslexic pornographer fills my e-mail Inbox with offers of "Hrony Grils" and cheap "Vigara," he has yet to advertise an Eternal O.

I can just hear Peter now: " 'Eternal O' would be a good name for a band."

By adult standards children can sustain rapture for quite a while, but even they can't make it last indefinitely. My daughter Woolie, for example, always looked forward to Halloween. To her, it sounded like an occasion of limitless rapture. Imagine! All the candy you could possibly want—talk about heaven! She counted down the days.

The magic moment finally arrived. Woolie went out into the night and returned, her cheeks pink with excitement under the face paint, her grocery sack bulging with loot. She carefully sorted the treasure on the living room carpet: all the candy bars in one pile, the Life Savers in another, the Dubble Bubble, the chocolate coins, the candy necklaces, the Necco Wafers . . . At last, hands trembling, she selected a fun size Almond Joy, peeled off the wrapper, and bit into it. Hallelujah!

She went on to gobble a handful of candy corn, savored six Starburst fruit chews, munched a Snickers bar—you could see the excitement fading. But a sense of workmanlike discipline kept her going. She ate a Reese's peanut butter cup and a Charleston Chew. She ate a red hot Atomic Fireball. Grimly, she slurped on a set of wax lips, managed one more Tootsie Pop, one more Hershey's kiss.

With that kiss, it was over. Woolie was sick to her stomach. Groaning and pale, she swore never to touch another sweet thing again as long as she lived. Another year, another repetition of Halloween's harsh lesson in the first of Buddha's four noble truths: Life is suffering. Pleasure is fleeting. Sweetness turns bitter. Joy doesn't last.

So picture poor old Osama, lolling under the date palms by the river of wine with his virgins. He has a bellyache from all the dates; he's sick of Chablis. The virgins all want to talk about their relationship issues forever and ever.

Life is suffering. And if it's life, then eternal life must be suffering too.

"I don't want to live forever," one of my seminary classmates proclaimed. "I'm tired of myself already!"

I know just what she means. Spend forever with myself? I mean, really! Look, I have quirks. I have eccentricities. I've learned, over the years, to tolerate myself well enough, but eternity is a long time to spend with someone who, for all her good qualities, talks a lot, is a compulsive knitter, and can't keep track of car keys.

And eternity is a long time to carry certain images around. The image of my husband's body in a coffin, for example, or of the backyard brush fire a few summers ago that, for a moment at least, seemed to have taken my children away from me.

Of course, maybe in heaven it will be given unto me to stop jabbering, to stop missing Drew and fearing fire. The heavenly me will never knit the sleeves too long on a sweater, never be crabby or idiotic or afraid. Maybe in heaven I will be perfect and perfectly happy.

But if I'm perfect and perfectly happy, I won't be me. And if I'm not me in heaven, not Kate Braestrup, the same Kate

Braestrup presently writing these words, then Kate Braestrup will be dead.

I have to say, Jesus is no help on this issue. He never talks about heaven directly. He says things like "In my Father's house are many mansions" (John 14:2), and "the kingdom of God is like a grain of mustard seed" (Mark 4:31), and "the kingdom of heaven is like yeast, mixed in with flour" (Mat. 13:33). These do not sound like the remarks of one who has the architecture and geography of a place laid out neatly in his mind. And why would he? When Jesus offered his parables about heaven, he wasn't talking about how we die, but about how we live.

My son Zach is the child of Unitarian Universalists, so naturally he didn't know a lot about Jesus. But I heard a lot about Jesus at my Christian seminary, and a lot of it was pretty cool. So one day, I found myself telling Zach about Jesus's life and death, the stories they told about him, what he said to his disciples.

"When Jesus talked about loving," I said, "I think he meant something really radical. I think he was talking about loving as God loves; loving completely, loving with a whole self. He told his disciples to give everything they had, everything they were, to hold nothing back, not money, not time, not even life itself. Everything was to be given over in the service of love."

I went on about this for a while, sermonizing in a motherly sort of way, and Zach listened carefully, because even as a young boy he was always a careful listener.

"So, Mom," he said at last. "Let's say I decide to become a devoted follower of Jesus Christ."

"What?" I said, startled and alarmed.

"No, but let's say I do."

"Okay," I said cautiously.

"And I die, and because I'm a Christian, I get to go to heaven instead of going to hell."

"Yeah . . ."

"If I really take Jesus seriously, if I really am willing to give up everything I am and everything I have in the service of love, *if I am really a Christian* . . . it seems to me I would have to give my place in heaven to someone else, someone who otherwise wouldn't get to go."

I stared at him.

"I'd have to go to hell, so this other person could be in heaven. Right, Mom?"

If you want my considered opinion on what actually happens to us when we die, I have to tell you, I think we just die. I think we cease to exist, in any way, shape, or form, except for the memories we leave behind with those who are still living. This has the starchy sound of certitude, as if I could cite research to back up my conclusions, but in fact heaven can't be proved or disproved in a lab. So my lack of interest in any afterlife whatsoever is doubtless driven by my own desires and fears. I don't want to live forever. I'm sick of myself already.

Sometimes I remember something funny that Drew once said, some offhand comment that still cracks me up, and I think: *Ah! To be able to make someone I love laugh years after I'm gone, that is all the immortality I could ever ask for.*

But what if I'm wrong?

Let's say you die, and then you *don't* die?

And there's heaven and hell and purgatory and all the rest of it, then what?

That's when I think about Zach's interpretation of Jesus's message: If you are, in Christian terms, following Christ, or in Unitarian Universalist terms, completely and wholly in love, then you are in heaven no matter where you are. If you are not in love, you are in hell, no matter where you are.

The stories we tell of heaven and hell are not about how we die, but about how we live.

Two summers ago, Woolie and Zach were badly burned when the gasoline my cousin George was using to ignite a pile of backyard brush essentially exploded in their faces. Being burned in a fire is one of the classic images of hell, and it's a pretty powerful one. Being burned hurts a lot.

As I drove my burned loved ones to the hospital, I had the 911 dispatcher on the cell phone. She kept asking me whether anyone was having trouble breathing. What she knew and

I didn't was that if George and the kids had inhaled the scalding air at the moment of ignition, the insides of their lungs would begin to swell and shred, and they could die very quickly.

So she kept saying, "Are they breathing?" And I would hold the cell phone up in the air, so she could hear the hellish sounds of them cursing and crying.

George was cursing and crying because his burns hurt and because he knew that the fire that had injured these children was his mistake, his fault. He was the adult who had decided to use gasoline to start the fire, and his was the hand that struck the match.

"Are they breathing?" the dispatcher said, and I held up the cell phone.

George, beside me in the passenger seat, said, "Oh my God. Oh hell. I am so sorry. I am so sorry."

Zach was sitting behind him in the backseat. In the middle of his own loud litany of "Oh God" and "Oh hell," Zach leaned forward. He reached out with his burned arm, an arm blistering and shredding before my eyes, and put his burned hand on George's shoulder.

"It's all right, George," he said. "We love you."

If you are living in love, you are in heaven no matter where you are. May heaven hold you. May you always, *always,* live in love.

CHAPTER THIRTEEN

I'm not really religious," Warden Hannah Robitaille told me. "But I did pray once."

"Ah," I said encouragingly, settling in for a story.

"I was on my way to one of the remote warden camps by Clayton Lake. The easiest way to get there is to drive as far as you can, then put your canoe into the water or your snowmobile onto the ice, and go directly across the lake to the camp on the far shore. It was January, and probably about negative two, so I brought my snowmobile. I had all my supplies, the tools I needed to do some repairs at the camp, all my food for a couple of days. I got maybe two-thirds of the way across that lake—we're talking eight miles? ten?—and the engine just dies. Conks out."

Hannah paused to sip her coffee and allow the ominous implications of this narrative turn to sink in.

"That's not good," I prodded her.

"Not good at all. It was really, really cold. Dark night,

snowing. I farted around for a little while, checking the spark plugs, twiddling some wires, but I couldn't do much with my mittens on, and if I took them off, my hands would freeze. So I think okay, screw this, I'm just going to walk. I put on all my extra clothes, get as much stuff as I can into my pack, check my direction on my compass so I'll be able to stay on course and find the camp, because now it's snowing so frigging hard, I can't see anything more than twenty feet away. I start walking.

"I figured out later it must have been four or five miles. With the wind howling and the snow blowing so hard, it's packing behind my glasses, and I have to dig the snow out of my eye sockets to take a compass reading. The nearest person—forget the nearest game warden—the nearest *human being* is like forty miles away."

"That was when you prayed, I'd guess?"

"Yeah. But the thing is, Kate, I wasn't afraid. I wasn't praying for help or anything. I was thankful. I was thinking, *God, this is great: I'm getting paid for this!*"

"You're nuts," I told her, laughing.

"Not that I wasn't glad to see the camp," Hannah said thoughtfully. "And I was glad to get home to my hubby too."

"Of course."

"But it was great," she said. "It really was."

Like wolves and deer, human beings are social beings. We don't function well without companions, and a person can literally die of loneliness. Still, most of us have at least some need for solitude. Like the Desert Fathers of early Christianity, like

Jesus and Buddha and Muhammad, some of us, at least, will actively seek isolation in the loneliest of landscapes, in the wild place beyond the Jordan where the crowds cannot find us.

A forest ranger from Acadia National Park told me about a new and irritating form of vandalism. People pick up rocks and make piles and patterns out of them. "Rock graffiti," it has been called, and these creations confuse hikers, who are usually guided by the park's own official rock cairns. But, as this ranger put it, they also "destroy the integrity of the natural landscape." Rocks arranged by a human being in the shape of a peace sign are not the same as rocks scattered naturally by a glacier, even if the rocks are identical and have only been moved a few feet in one direction or another.

On one level, of course, I agree with the ranger; the rock graffiti artists ought to knock it off. Organisms living under stones deserve to live their tiny lives undisturbed. And besides, when I go into the wilderness, I want it to look like wilderness. I want the illusion that I am going where no one else has gone before. Still, it's sort of touching the way human beings go off into the wilderness to be alone and then can't resist communicating with anyone who might come along afterward: Are you here? I was here too! Peace, dude!

Every year, someone who goes off into the wilderness realizes, one way or another, that he can't find his way out. Communion with the natural world changes its flavor when it becomes involuntary and, apparently, interminable. In such situations, the human ear attunes itself acutely to sounds that might indicate the suddenly welcome presence of people: engines, voices, the cheerful bark of a domesticated dog. Then it would be great to find a rock peace sign or better still, a nice camp with a fireplace and a telephone.

"I'll never go out there again," they promise, when the wardens finally find them and bring them home.

Hannah told me that the time she spent walking through the blizzard on the lake, miles from nowhere, was the most joyous time of her whole life, yet she was pleased when it ended. There it is, another spiritual paradox.

Human beings want to live in community, and so we want ours to be an intimate universe presided over by a Father God who cares for us and whose universe is responsive to us. At the same time, we are drawn out of community and physically experience a harsh and lonely cosmos in whose vastness stars are born and explode, and solar systems come into being and fall apart. Closer to home, continents swim around like bits of eggshell on the molten yolk of our planet, banging into one another, squashing the earth's crust into mountains that promptly erode into the sea. It is a universe in which our soft bodies can be fried or frozen, parched or drowned or dashed against a stone. Seekers of truth, when confronted by such cosmic indifference, can find it both frightening and liberating.

Like the game wardens, I understand what draws New Age hikers, enlightenment hunters, and even the deeply depressed out beyond the comfortable edge of the human-centered world, out to where moose, woodcock, grouse, and mink live without reference to the human, out to where a person does not matter at all. The air will be as warm or as cold, as dry or as damp as the indifferent physics of front meeting front demands. Pray or don't pray. Ask and ye shall receive what you would have received without asking: succor that comes in time or doesn't.

Chipmunks scooted past as Betsy, the young suicidal mother, staggered and fell into the yellow leaves to sleep away the remaining minutes of her life.

Chickadees peeped and chattered companionably to one another in the trees as Eddie Seavey tore his clothing from his body and exposed his naked skin to icy air that felt to him, in its indifference and lethality, like fire.

No human help for miles and miles, the air thick with snow and impossible to see through. It was hard to breathe. Standing on the frozen surface of Clayton Lake, a lone game warden, unobserved, exulted.

I am sympathetic. I too want wildness, the existential freedom, the release and exaltation of being in and of a world in which humanity is only one dimension of the whole.

But then I want it to end. If I am lost, I want the wardens to come find me. And if I am dead, I want someone to pray for me, even if my head has become a tempting toy for bears, my flesh a welcome resource for creatures fattening up for winter. The chickadees don't have to pray. The bears can have their ball, but if a member of my species should happen to find me, or merely a sign I've left behind, a bent twig, a pile of stones, words, perhaps they will be so kind as to say a prayer and cry a little on the way home from the search.

Chapter Fourteen

Mom-Dude!" Peter announced. "I need you to drive me to Appleton. I bought drums."

"What are you talking about?"

"Drums, Mom!" He did a little Ringo Starr pantomime. "You know, drums? Ned Rich says I can join his band."

"But you don't know how to play the drums, do you?" Did he? I wracked my brain. There had been guitar lessons, karate class, a pretty Japanese tutor named Kyoko that Peter still considered his ideal woman, but I recalled no drums.

Peter was giving me a look of pained condescension.

"I'm going to buy the drums, and then I'm going to learn to play them," he said, enunciating clearly, in deference to his mother's evident stupidity.

This didn't sound like a particularly promising plan to me, but Peter had spent his own money on the project, and he swore up and down that he wouldn't play too loud, or after nine o'clock, and that he would stop immediately if our neighbor Mrs. Pinkham complained.

So Peter and I drove to Appleton. Smiling with grim satisfaction, the parents of the drums' previous owner watched us load them into the back of my car. Over the next few months, I would periodically hear Peter banging away up in his room, and I'd yell, "Knock that off! It's nine fifteen!" This was the sum total of my contribution to Peter's musical career. About six months later, I was at a school function—something to do with congratulating the basketball team on a fine season, I think—and lo and behold, there was Peter, up on stage with his friends, and he was playing, actually playing, the drums.

"He's gotten really good!" one of the other mothers shouted at me, above the amplified sound of the band Peter was now clearly part of. "I didn't know your son could play so well!"

Well? I didn't know my son could play *at all*.

It was one of the many discouraging moments of my single parenthood. *God, I am such an awful parent*, I thought. *My son is playing drums in a rock-and-roll band, and he's damned good, and obviously loves it, and I knew nothing about it.*

I was halfway home from the search for Betsy, the suicidal mother, thinking about Peter. I was driving along a road that winds through a salt marsh below the hamlet of Frankfurt, when a duck flew up and over me, just clearing the car. The windshield wipers cleared an arc in time for me to glimpse its fawn-colored underbelly, the muscles in its eager breast working, its very orange feet treading the air. "Hello, duck!" I exclaimed aloud in the car, suddenly sensing, in my own body, its avian urgency, its terror and wild hope. And that was when—alone in the car—I finally began to cry.

Lots of cops cry on the way home from scenes. Women officers cry more easily than men, not because they are weaker, but because for them the release of tears is both socially and physiologically permitted at a lower level of distress. But men will admit, at least to their chaplain, that the driver's seat of their cruiser or truck is where they mourn those deaths that have found, for whatever reason, the chinks in the armor they otherwise maintain.

Warden Robitaille told me that there was an infant safety seat in the car that Betsy left behind when she went off to die, for example. While I could look at Betsy's body—to this day, it is not an image I shy away from—I refused to go and have a look at that infant seat. It was the mere idea of the infant seat that got me, that and the duck's eager orange feet. Oh, and the blue journal, and the fact that I, the plucky widow, didn't even know that my son Peter could play the drums. These things made me cry that day.

"At least we found her," Lieutenant Trisdale said of Betsy. "Don't I hate it when we never do find the body? It doesn't happen often, but it does happen, and it eats at you."

The warden service spent five long days coordinating a search through thick scrub woods, around and in water, through people's backyards and farmyards, but the "subject" never turned up. He had been taking drugs, though what sort of drugs was never made completely clear.

"He didn't inject," his girlfriend insisted.

She sat nervously on the storage box that served as a bench. We were in the overhead team's search and rescue trailer, with the familiar laptops glowing blue, the search areas carefully marked out on the topographical maps Nate Robertson had installed. The girlfriend's tummy spilled out above the tight hipline of her jeans, exposing a recently pierced umbilicus. It looked irritated and red.

"Me and him, neither of us would ever, ever inject. No way." She said it with a curious self-righteousness, as if the mode of delivery made all the difference in the moral standing of a junkie.

It was bound to be a difficult search: a witness noted an erratic gait and queer expression when Jason staggered across her back lawn on his way to the woods beyond, and it is always difficult to predict what a drugged or otherwise neurologically impaired subject will do. On the other hand, given his involvement in the local illegal drug trade, fleeing the murderous intentions of a former business associate, his odd behavior might have been the result of a sheer and well-justified terror. Or he could have been putting on a show, faking his own disappearance and apparent demise so as to permanently escape the criminal charges that were pending. Or he could just be lost in the woods, for ordinary reasons unrelated to either his addictions or his line of work.

"You know," Nate said casually, resting one haunch on

the corner of the computer desk. "I've never really taken recreational drugs. None of us has, except for Reverend Braestrup here, and she doesn't remember much." Nate said it deadpan, and the girlfriend turned to look at me, wide-eyed.

I shrugged. "I was young," I said, and Nate permitted himself a small smile.

"The thing is, it could really help us if we had a sense of what drugs he might have taken, and what effect they might have on him."

"Like what?" the girl asked suspiciously. "You know, I'm not going to say anything that might get Jason in trouble."

"Jason's already in trouble. The last time anyone saw him, he was acting extremely disorientated and paranoid, and he looked sick. He's not going to be able to take good care of himself if he's out in the woods in that condition. Right now, we're not interested in a prosecution. Right now, we just want to find your boyfriend alive, as I'm sure you do."

"He wasn't injecting," the girlfriend assured us. "Maybe speedballing," she said, glancing sideways at us as if to gauge our disapproval. "I don't really know. I'm not his mother."

"Speedballing. That's what—cocaine and heroin?" Nate asked. "So what do you think? You've seen him stoned before. Would he keep moving or conk out? Would he want another fix at some point, badly enough to come out of the woods to get it? Would he hallucinate?"

The girlfriend thought about it for a long moment while we waited. "One time," she said, absently fingering the ring in her sore, red navel, "I thought I was, like, a glass of orange juice sitting on a counter. I mean, it was so real. And I was scared, like, shitless because someone could come and knock me over and everything would, like, spill out."

"Huh," said Nate. "And was that from speedballing?"

"I can't recall," the girlfriend admitted. "Maybe acid."

A warden peeked his head around the door and announced the arrival of a psychic. Nate shot me a look. "I've got it," I said.

The psychic had driven all the way from Waterville to inform us that Jason was being held against his will.

"Really?" I said. "By whom?"

"I can't tell," the psychic said, frowning. "Evil guys, though, for sure." She had dyed blond hair and blue, exophthalmic eyes accentuated with plenty of eye shadow. The eye shadow sparkled in the summer sun. Fish scales are used to make cosmetics shine, I remembered, irrelevantly. Cochineal pigment, which makes lipstick red, is made from bug blood. The things we smear on ourselves without knowing it . . .

"They might be terrorists," the psychic was saying. "Y'know? Like, Arabian terrorists? And there's definitely some kind of construction site near the place where they've got him tied up . . . like, big machinery, y'know, plus I'm getting a wicked strong sense about Connecticut."

"Connecticut?"

"Yeah."

"You mean he's *in* Connecticut?"

"He could be. Unless he was born there or, like, thinks about it a lot . . . I don't know. But I'm getting a strong feeling about Connecticut. I thought you people should know."

I thanked her and went off to fetch some antibiotic ointment from the first aid kit in my truck. I offered it to the girlfriend for her infected belly button, but she declined. "I'm into, like, homeopathy," she said. "It's more natural."

"The psychic is sure that he's being held against his will at a construction site in Connecticut," I told Nate. He snorted.

"Then the one thing we know for sure is that he isn't anywhere near any construction sites," Nate said. "And we can probably take the whole of southern New England out of the BOLO [be-on-the-lookout] zone. What a relief."

"Has a psychic ever proved useful?" I asked.

"Never. They are always, always, always wrong. And no matter how off-the-mark they are, it never seems to faze them. They keep showing up with their useless dreams and gut feelings and visions. I keep hoping that one of these so-called psychics might just be a citizen who has good information he or she doesn't want to come out with directly. Right? Susie So-and-So has a suspicion about her peculiar Uncle Joe, but she doesn't want to piss off his family by naming him. So she'll say, 'Oh, I had a dream that the victim was on a lobster boat with red gunwales,' and hope we'll take her seriously enough to have a look at Joe's boat. So far, this theory hasn't played out in any search I've been part of. The psychics are always outsiders. They are always wrong. They upset and confuse the victim's family. And they make things harder. But I do let them have their say, just in case." Sure enough.

"You keep questioning me about what Jason's using," his girlfriend said angrily the next time Nate interviewed her. "He's, like, a hostage. That lady said she works with cops all the time. Why aren't you guys working with her? You should be looking for Jason in Connecticut instead of screwing around here."

Nate assured her that Jason's description had been distributed to law enforcement agencies throughout New England and that the Connecticut police would keep their eyes open.

"This whole search seems like a waste of time to me," she said disdainfully as she left.

As it turned out, Jason never reappeared. Perhaps this was the one time a psychic got it right, and there's a terrorist cell in New London that has a drug dealer's abduction to answer for.

While it was possible, as one of the more cynical wardens suggested, that Jason's girlfriend was deliberately playing the role of frantic loved one to cover his escape, I was inclined to believe her when she said tearfully, "I miss him so much. Why won't he come home?"

"Aw, honey," I said, and after a while she did, at least, let me put some Bacitracin on her belly button.

"She thought she was a glass of orange juice, and that someone was going to spill her," Nate reflected later. "And my kids wonder why I'm so paranoid about drugs?"

The disappearance of the drug-addled young man was only the most obvious example of a tragedy with substance abuse at its root. Many if not most of the deaths I see are caused at least in part by drug or alcohol use. Here's a sobering, personal statistic: in as many years, I have responded to five deaths of people who drowned in water shallow enough to stand in, had they only been sober enough to stand.

I do not address root causes. I am, in the parlance of law enforcement, reactive rather than proactive. For the most part, I show up after an accident has happened. The skull has fractured, the lungs have filled with water, the end is near or nearing. If I were to address root causes, I would stand on a street corner in Augusta, or Portland, or Billerica, Massachusetts (home to a mysteriously large proportion of our outdoor recreation casualties), shouting these words in the tone and with the urgency of Bible Blasters who bellow Revelation from memory:

Do not drink and swim!

Do not drink and operate a boat, canoe, ATV, or snowmobile!

Do not drink and attempt to work through your relationship issues!

Do not drink!

"Don't drink!" I tell my children.

I am falling prey to one of the occupational hazards of the law enforcement parent: I'm paranoid. None of my kids is allowed to so much as look at a snowmobile or an ATV. I force them to wear helmets for everything I can think of—bicycling, skiing, skateboarding, walking to the store. I watch them swim with a newly nervous eye, counting heads—one, two, three, four . . . one, two, three, four—over and over, and if I had my druthers, they'd wear personal flotation devices in the shower. I do this even though the boys have grown taller and stronger than I am and Ellie and Woolie are close behind. Tall, strong boys drown too. I have been there when they pull out the bodies, the muscled arms and knees bent at the drowner's characteristic angle, as if the strong boy died in the middle of a subaqueous genuflection.

As my sons enter adolescence, I lecture them endlessly about drinking and drugs: "The victim staggered into the water, fell over, and was too drunk to get to his feet," I tell them. "That is a stupid way to die. Do you hear me? Don't die that way."

Yeah, yeah.

"Peter!" I insist. "Don't die!"

"Mom-Dude," Peter says, towering over me, hugging me around my head and crushing my ear affectionately to his sternum. I can hear his heart beating. "Peace, Mom-Dude."

Chapter Fifteen

Disregard," the Augusta dispatcher advised with relief in her voice over the radio, canceling my next call out. The first trooper on scene had swiftly located the missing toddler. The toddler was in the backyard, tangled in the dog's chain, hysterical but unhurt. No one was dead. I could turn my car around and go home. *Thanks be to God.*

"Is your job dangerous?" Ellie asked me.

"Of course not, Ellie-Belly," I said.

"Then why do you have to wear a bulletproof vest?"

Ellie had claimed the middle of my bed. It was, she explained, the only quiet place in the house in which to do her math homework. Naturally her brother followed her into my room, having discovered in himself a sudden yen for maternal wisdom. Did I have any suggestions about what to name his new rock group?

"How about Redundant Male?" Ellie offered. Peter had

been about to retort in kind when I pulled the vest out of my gear bag. That distracted them both.

"That is so unbelievably way cool," Peter said. "Can I wear it to school?"

I pressed the front Kevlar panel to my chest and adjusted the Velcro straps around my bosom and flab. "No, Peter," I said. "And it's not actually a bulletproof vest, Ellie."

"What would you call it then?"

Edna, in supply, had informed me that she prefers *ballistic vest* or *body armor* because the vest won't stop rounds from certain kinds of weapons. "So it isn't really accurate to call it *bulletproof,*" Edna said. "And of course, an edged weapon can penetrate Kevlar," she warned. "That's why there's this steel-plate supplement over the area of the heart."

A discourse on the limitations of miracle fibers was not what Ellie was asking for. My daughter is calm and smart, which often makes her seem older than she is. But she was only thirteen, and she had already lost one parent.

It would not comfort her to know that the federal government has declared law enforcement chaplains eligible for federal death benefits should they die on the job, or that the wardens have pledged to stuff me into my uniform and drag my body into the woods should ill health or my own poor judgment lead me to die 10-7 (off-duty).

"It's called body armor, honey. Chaplains' organizations now recommend that all law enforcement chaplains be issued a vest. So Colonel Santaguida gave me this one. It's a used vest," I assured her, as if that made a difference. "It used to be Cheryl Barden's before she retired. And it's not like I have to actually wear it . . . much. In fact, I *can't* wear it, for the most part. My torso is a tool of my trade, after all. People hug me. My body has to be soft and squishy."

"Can I try it on?" Peter asked again. "And try stabbing myself?"

"No." I took off the vest and stuffed it into one of the several large canvas bags I use to organize my gear. I covered it with the fleece sweater I also inherited from Cheryl.

The vest will almost certainly remain there, unused, ready to be handed on to the next chaplain who comes along, provided she's female and a size 6/8.

"It's important to get a proper fit around the armpits," Edna had said. "If you leave gaps, the bullet could get in there and wind up banging around inside of you, and you don't want that."

"It's a woman's vest," I told Peter. "It wouldn't fit you properly."

It seems ridiculous to have this vest and just as ridiculous to pretend it's something other than it is. It feels like just so much melodrama: my job really *isn't* dangerous, at least, not in the sense that I am likely to be exposed to small-arms fire.

I resisted the notion that a chaplain should wear body armor until Warden Mike Pierre told me about a dicey death notification he participated in a few years before I came on the job. The victim had been shot while hunting with a large group of friends and was rushed to the hospital in critical condition. His friends repaired to their hunting camp to blunt the edge of their distress with large doses of coffee brandy. Hours later, Mike was sent to the hunting camp to inform these well-armed, very drunk men not only that the victim had died but also that the bullet that killed him had come from his best friend's gun. Had I been the chaplain at the time, I would have gone with Mike to do the notification.

"I would have felt a lot more comfortable having you with me if you had a vest on," Mike said. "Just in case." *If it makes the wardens happy, I'll do it,* I told myself resignedly.

Still, the most dangerous thing I do as a chaplain is also the most dangerous thing Mike does as a game warden. Statistically speaking, it was the most dangerous thing Drew ever did as a state trooper and is doubtless the most dangerous thing you do too. We drive.

I am on the road at all hours of the day and night. Sometimes I drive while distracted, adrenalized, or exhausted. Occasionally, I am a passenger in a pickup truck going eighty or ninety miles an hour along narrow roads. Even with blue lights and a wailing siren, it is dangerous.

"Why don't these people get out of the way?" I asked Warden Nate Robertson one afternoon. "Don't they know they're supposed to yield to emergency vehicles?"

Nate shrugged. Recently promoted, he was too busy considering the manifold responsibilities awaiting him at the scene to bother commenting on such a commonplace irritant.

The call had come in as a swimming accident. Two bathers had gone over a waterfall at a state park, splashing down in a deep, rock-studded gorge. One was dead at the scene; the other was badly injured. "They're still in the water," the dispatcher said.

"That doesn't sound good," Nate replied.

"Twenty-one twenty-three, Skowhegan FD is on scene, twenty-one fifty-one wants to know if you want ten fifty-six."

Nate considered for a moment. "Twenty-one twenty-three, Augusta . . . Ah, if twenty-one fifty-one thinks we need a helicopter from the National Guard to extract, we should go ahead and make the request, ten three?"

"Ten four."

Nate inhaled and exhaled long and forcefully, puffing his cheeks. All the wardens seem to do this when they are in a state of heightened tension. I've caught myself doing it—a deep breath and a good long blow—in stressful circumstances. In my case, it's usually while I'm waiting to preside over a particularly sorrowful funeral. *May the words of my mouth and the meditations of my heart be acceptable to you, my Lord and my God . . .*

I am never anxious enough to puff this way when I'm on an airboat skidding sideways across the surface of a river, or when I'm in the warden service airplane as it skis to a landing on a frozen lake. And maybe I'm too stupid to huff and blow, too dumb to know how much danger I'm in as we drive, lights flashing and siren blaring, over the winding, hilly roads of Maine. I, of all people, should know that.

Nate and I made it to the state park in one piece. He

pulled a backpack from his rear seat and checked to be sure he had what he needed: flashlights, flares, ropes, an extra Leatherman tool, first aid kit, protein bars, the policies and procedures manual, various forms, useful phone numbers, an extra cell phone battery, a water bottle. I had my mini-Bibles in my pocket and a Kleenex. I was good to go.

We hiked a mile and a half through the woods. A sibilant, watery whisper rose to thunder as we drew near, and the warm air by the river was thick with moisture. Mosquitoes gathered in blissful throngs. I bummed some insect repellant from Nate.

"It's organic," he warned. "We'll have to slop it on again in fifteen minutes."

Several wardens were already there, and a local fire department had deployed something their chief proudly described as a "vertical descent alpine rescue team."

"It's a new thing for us," the chief told me. "Because of all the ski resorts around here, we got a grant for the equipment and the training. When a skier goes flying off into a gully, we've got what we need to pull 'em out."

Five buff firefighters were busy arranging a complex web of ropes and pulleys on a patch of level ground. Lines extended from the rope web and disappeared over the fern-fringed edge of the chasm. Some teenage swimmers were standing around rubbernecking, so a warden mustered them into pulling teams. The fire chief winced when the teenagers touched the ropes.

"We're still new at this," he explained. "This is the first time we've done a vertical rescue for real. I don't mind telling you, I'm glad somebody's here to pray for us."

"Your people look like they know what they're doing," I said encouragingly.

"Ah, they've been chomping at the bit, hoping for a chance to try it all out," the fire chief said. "They're good boys, and they train hard. I want it all to go right for them. And for that poor lady down there too, of course," he added hastily.

"Is the body of the other victim still down there?"

"Still there. He'll have to wait. He can't get any more dead than he is right now, and the lady's supposed to meet the LifeFlight helicopter at that field opposite the park entrance."

"Do you know what her injuries are?"

"Ah, she's pretty well buggered up. The climber down there with her says compound fracture of one arm, probably at least one broken leg and maybe a broken pelvis, and I don't know what else. Go over a waterfall and you're not going to go dancing that night."

"I suppose not. How did she manage not to drown?"

"One witness said he saw the guy holding her head out of the water. If that's the case, I don't know how he managed; he was bleeding out. I mean, that water was all red, even with the current moving it on downstream. Hey, jeez, do you know if any of your guys have an ATV with 'em?"

"Adam—the tall guy there—has one on the back of his truck. But isn't the National Guard helicopter coming?"

"Yes, but their ETA is over an hour. This lady isn't going

to want to wait that long. And it's two miles to the park entrance, some rough ground there, and I'm thinking, realistically, we can't carry her that far." The chief went off to consult with the warden.

"When I give you the signal, you pull on this rope here," Warden Adam Kelly was explaining to the teenagers. "You don't pull on any other ropes, just this one. Got it?" The kids nodded nervously, twiddling the rope between their fingers. One boy's fashionably low-slung surf shorts revealed a large green cannabis leaf tattooed on his left ass cheek.

"Pull hard," the warden said. "But not till I tell you."

The teenagers' eyes were glued to the edge of the gorge where a couple of firefighters crouched among lush ferns, bright orange safety lines anchoring them to nearby trees. They leaned out into the abyss, into the fine spray thrown up by the waterfall, and shouted and signed to an unseen rescuer below.

"Okay, pull," one of the firefighters called from the edge.

"*Pull*, boys!" the chief roared. The teenagers braced their flip-flops in the mud and pulled.

The ropes twined and whirred. Game wardens and firefighters joined the teens, and in no time, the green ferns parted to reveal the bright orange bottom of a stiff fiberglass stretcher tipping up over the lip of the gorge. It was accompanied by a climber in a red helmet.

"Hold!" the chief commanded. "Good job, men. Good job. Hold it there."

The climber made a few adjustments to the ropes. The

woman on the stretcher, still hanging nearly vertically in her plastic bed, gave an audible yelp, and the climber smiled at her.

"Atta girl, Mona," he said. "You're almost there."

Another heave, and the stretcher—its occupant trussed up as thoroughly as a Lakota papoose—came to rest on level ground. The injured woman endured a brief examination by a paramedic, then six sweaty men bore her away, up a rise toward the main trail where the warden's ATV waited. Somehow—don't ask me how—the stretcher was bound with ropes and bungee cords to the ATV, which then jostled and bumped over the rough trails to a little dirt road, where Mona was transferred to the bed of a warden's pickup truck and driven to the park entrance. There she was transferred again, this time to the LifeFlight helicopter, which flew her to a hospital in Lewiston.

Extracting the dead man was a somewhat different process. Though he remained in the water while the complex logistics of evacuating the living were enacted, he didn't get any more dead, just as the chief had predicted. Eventually, buoyed with extra life jackets, the body was maneuvered downstream through the rapids to a place where the high, steep cliff walls gave way to a more moderate sloping bank. The rope web was redeployed, and the body was hauled out. It was examined both for a cause of death ("large open wound on right side/complete exsanguination") and for identifying marks. His face was compared to the driver's license found with the clothing and wallets on shore. Face and photo matched; the dead man's name was Fred Shilenski, and he was from Billerica, Massachusetts.

It was just as well that the National Guard helicopter was already in the air and en route; the day was getting on, and it would have been very difficult to carry the body over land before darkness fell.

"Our chaplain is going to say a prayer," Nate announced. He took off his cap. The wardens bowed their heads, and the assembled firefighters, teenagers, and paramedics glanced shyly at one another, then followed suit, their hands folded in front of their climbing harnesses, sweat-stained T-shirts, and bare chests.

I knelt in the mud beside the plastic stretcher and laid a suddenly tender hand on the dead man's head. "Receive and bless the spirit of this man, Fred Shilenski, as the waters have received his blood, as the earth will receive his body. Bless the sorrowing hearts of those who love him. Lend skill and strength to the hands of those who would heal his friend Mona. Amen."

"Amen," the assembled chorused.

"That was nice," the boy with the pot leaf on his butt told me, but Nate was already shooing him off with the others.

"Appreciate it, buddy, but you need to get moving. I need all nonessential personnel out of here by the time the chopper arrives."

I couldn't claim to be essential, but Nate was my ride home, so I stayed. Nate dismissed all but a half dozen game wardens, then insisted that only he remain with the corpse to greet the chopper. Everyone else was ordered to withdraw to what he considered a safe distance.

"Like, down there," he said, pointing down the trail. "No, *farther* down!" he shouted, when we hadn't gone far enough. "And clear the area!"

I had been on hand on other occasions when the National Guard lent assistance to warden service ground searches and, while a Black Hawk is a large and impressively loud aircraft, I had never felt personally threatened by one flying over the command post or landing in a nearby field.

"Do we really need to move stuff this large?" I panted, setting down my portion of a heavy spare stretcher. My partner, a young warden, rolled his eyes. "Nate's become a granny since he got promoted," he muttered. We could hear the distant *whup, whup, whup* of the approaching helicopter.

Still, the warden service is not a democracy. Because the sergeant said so, the wardens and I moved backpacks, water bottles, ropes, a rock hammer, and other stray bits of loose equipment down the trail while the *whup, whup, whup* got louder.

A stiff breeze began to move through the forest, and the stout tree trunks creaked alarmingly. Little rocks stirred around my boots. Up the trail, Nate crouched alone beside the stretcher. He peered intently skyward through the flailing branches. An overlooked water bottle, half empty, took to the air and flew past his face. *Whup, whup, whup. WHUP, WHUP, WHUP.*

You know those videos they show on the Weather Channel, the ones of category four hurricanes making landfall? That's what being in the woods under the downwash of a Black Hawk is like.

As the helicopter descends, thick pines bend double, and a strong, young game warden finds he can barely keep his feet. He turns to his chaplain, wide-eyed and chastened, and shouts, "Maybe we should move a little farther away?"

So we do. When we look back, the splintered trunk of a large birch is lying across the trail where we had just been standing.

"Is your job dangerous?" Ellie had asked me, her pencil poised above her algebra.

"I think Bulletproof Boobs would be a good name for a rock band," Peter mused.

A spidery thread emerged from the aircraft's belly. A metal basket stretcher attached to the end of the thread rotated slowly downward, followed by a soldier dangling casually from his own line.

The young warden explained that if I was ever in a position to receive a metal basket stretcher from a helicopter, I should let the basket hit the ground before I touch it. Apparently, a static charge builds up from the rotors, and if you touch the metal, you are electrocuted. I put my hands behind my back as if to shield them from temptation.

Watching nervously, I expected the charged basket to spark or judder when it met the mud, but it touched down with no more force or fanfare than a bread basket being placed on a dinner table. Whatever energy exchanged between it and earth did so discreetly.

In moments the soldier landed lightly too, unclipping himself from his harness and greeting Nate with a cheerful smile. He was skinny and blond. He looked very young and reminded me of Zach.

He released the tether from the basket stretcher, and the helicopter moved off to relieve us of the downwash while the body was transferred. The woods seemed comically quiet, the thunder of a waterfall a mere murmur compared to the Black Hawk's rotors.

"Wow, Nate," I said as we bent to lift the body. "That chopper is really something, isn't it?"

Nate's hat had vanished, and his cowlicks were all blown flat, making him look uncharacteristically well groomed.

"The chopper is *unreal*," I continued.

Nate grinned at me, then his soft, brown gaze suddenly sharpened. "Hey!" he snapped. "Blood-borne diseases!"

I was touching the body, gripping the bloody shirt with bare hands.

"Gloves," Nate reminded me.

I said "Sorry, Sergeant," humbly, and put mine on.

Fred Shilenski's body was pale and heavy, still soggy from the river. The gash on his right side gaped a little as we moved him, showing a solidifying edge of yellow fat, a brief gleam of gut, but no blood. There was no more blood.

What remained of Mr. Shilenski was wrapped in a body

bag and strapped for his ascent. The soldier radioed that all was ready, and this time the sergeant didn't need to urge a retreat. All nonessential personnel skedaddled. The Black Hawk returned, thrashing the forest.

The body left the earth and was lifted skyward. The soldier, again clipped to his long umbilical, followed. Even at a distance, his thin frame appeared relaxed as he ascended, one hand on the cord, the other resting on his harnessed hip. His blond head turned as he took in the view.

Two hours later, my eyes still red and gritty from the flying duff, my hair full of bark, my boots dropping mud on the clean linoleum of Central Maine Medical Center's ICU, I told Mona that her boyfriend didn't make it, that Fred was dead.

Immobilized by a cervical collar, intravenous lines, and painkillers, by the various pulleys that held her in traction, the casts on her left arm and right leg, and the steel bracing that kept her from further injuring her broken pelvis, Mona began to weep.

"It's my fault," she said.

Well, Ellie, I mused on the way home. *I suppose that on this single day, I might have been squashed by a flying birch tree, picked up hepatitis, or been infected with the iatrogenic streptococcus doubtless incubating all over the ICU. Or an inattentive driver—there are plenty of those—might have swerved in front of Nate's truck as we tore from one side of the state to the other.*

In fact, I might have fallen asleep at the wheel as I drove home from Lewiston at four o'clock in the morning.

"Mom-Dude!" Peter's message on my voicemail said. *"Barbed Wire Catheter!* What do you think?"

I guess my job does involve a not infrequent exposure to peculiar hazards. None of these could be eliminated by the ballistic vest now stored in the bowels of my gear bag. I could have admitted this to my daughter. Instead, I promised her airily and easily and probably truthfully that I wouldn't get shot.

"I don't really deal with criminals anyway," I told Ellie. "Just game wardens and victims of accidents."

"Of course it isn't your fault, honey," I reassured Mona. "How could it be?"

"It might have been murder," Fritz Trisdale informed me the next day. "I kid you not, Reverend Mother. We're turning the whole case over to the detectives at the Criminal Investigations Division. Mona told Nate when he interviewed her this morning that they went in the water for a cool dip. Said she got into trouble, was getting swept over the falls by the current, and hero Fred tried to save her."

"And?"

"And that's her story, Reverend Mother. But did you take a look at the area above the falls? That isn't a place anybody would think to swim, even if they were stoned or drunk, which Fred and Mona friggin' well were."

"Which—stoned or drunk?"

"She admitted straight out that they'd been drinking. Then she kept asking Nate whether they'd found her purse, whether anybody had looked in her purse. Finally Nate told her, Yeah we looked in the purse. We inventoried your cash. You have a hundred twenty-six dollars and fourteen cents in an envelope in the hospital safe, and lady, I personally threw your jeezly nickel bag in the Dumpster."

"Huh," I said thoughtfully.

"Of course, he said it in a professional manner. It's not like we're going to summons her for possession after all of this. But then we come to find out that the Billerica P.D. is on very familiar terms with Fred and Mona. Drug stuff, receiving stolen property, aggravated assault. I mean seriously, Katie, this pair had *history*."

I pictured Mona's tears trickling down her temples, soaking into her hair. How achingly pitiable she had been, trying to cry while prone, immobilized under the bright lights and video monitors of the ICU.

"Oh, Lieutenant," I said. "What a bummer."

"I'll tell you *what*. So now we're thinking maybe they drank and smoked themselves stupid, got into a fight, and she goes out into the water by the falls, saying she's going to throw herself over the edge, and he gets out there to yank her back, and she grabs onto him and slips . . . or jumps. Or maybe he dragged her out there himself and was going to chuck her off. Or maybe—what the hell—they made a pact, and both jumped together, hand in hand, who knows? But CID is treating this as a suspicious death. Which is nice for Nate— they can do the paperwork.

"So I called the guy's family this morning to tell them I'm

sorry, I have some bad news and so on and so forth. They didn't seem too broke up. After a lot of backin' and forthin', Fred's brother gave me the number for their local funeral parlor, but the undertaker won't take the case. Says he won't let Fred's body in the door until the family comes by and pays what they already owe him for embalming dear old Aunt Bernice.

"Are you laughing, Reverend Mother?"

I was, actually, in spite of myself.

"In cash, the guy said, because the Shilenskis' checks are *pure rubbah. Pure rubbah!*"

The lieutenant and I were both laughing now, the way one might as well laugh at awful things.

"Poor Shilenskis. And poor Mona."

"Well, you have to say that, I guess, being a religious woman. Bunch of oxygen thieves if you ask me. For these people, my guys risk their necks? And while we're on the subject, Your Holiness, I heard you were out there in the woods when the helicopter came for the body. Do we need to issue you a helmet?"

Sure, I thought, scratching the mosquito bite behind my ear. A helmet, a bulletproof (excuse me, *ballistic*) vest, purple puncture-resistant gloves, a hepatitis vaccine . . .

"Maybe some goggles," I said. "My eyelashes are still full of bark chips."

Receive his spirit as the water has received his blood, as the earth shall receive his body. . . . Would I have asked something else of God, if I had known for sure that Fred had tried to murder Mona, or been murdered by her, or if indeed they had clumsily conspired to end their unhappy story in mutual murder?

"Such a terrible, frightening day," I had said to Mona, stroking her hair, wiping her nose with my Kleenex, wanting so much to offer her at least the meager shelter of an embrace.

"It's all right to be sad," I told her. "You're safe now."

"It's my fault," she said.

"No, no," I soothed her. But maybe it truly was her fault?

Fred was dead, his body would lie unclaimed until someone ponied up the price of its disposal. Mona would go home to Billerica, where her arm would eventually be amputated at the elbow. Owing to her drug use, psychological instability, and physical incapacity, her daughter (who might or might not have been Fred's child) would be taken from her by the state. "The sun does rise upon the evil and the good, and the rain falls also on the just and on the unjust" (Mat. 5:45).

I wish I had stayed longer by Mona's bedside that night in the ICU, stroking her hair. I wish I had listened more attentively to what she was trying to tell me, for it might have been the truth.

As it was, I wiped her nose unknowing, too easily imagining that I had helped bring her, innocent, to safety.

Chapter Sixteen

What is his probable cause for *that* search, I'd like to know?"

It's a Friday night. I'm straddling the armrest of the couch with a Bible in one hand, a slice of pizza in the other. I'm almost done with my degree. The master's is so close, I can almost taste it. An assignment for a class in New Testament theology hangs over my head.

"Mom, shut up," Zach replies, his eyes glued to the video.

"He has to go in there. That's the criminal's hideout," Peter says.

"He still has to have a warrant. Anything he finds is going to be inadmissible."

"Yeah, but he's just going to blow up all the bad guys in the end," Peter reminds me calmly. "Bruce Willis doesn't go to court."

"Other people are *trying* to watch the *movie!*" Zach admonishes. "Gawd, Mom! Don't you have homework to do?"

Yes, as a matter of fact I do.

"Jesus was on his way to Jerusalem one day, when he was approached by ten lepers," I read to the girls. My assignment is from the Gospel of Luke (17:12–19), and I figure I might as well read parts of it aloud. Woolie receives the story with enthusiasm at first. But it turns out she thought Jesus was approached by ten leopards.

"Not leopards, honey, *lepers*. Lepers are people who have a horrible skin disease called leprosy."

"Oh," said Woolie, wrinkling her nose. This story wasn't going to be as interesting as she thought.

"So anyway," I went on, "when the lepers saw Jesus, they kept their distance, because they didn't want to gross him out with their yucky sores and missing fingers."

"Eew!"

"*Mother!*"

"But they did call out to him. 'Hey, Jesus!' they said. 'Master! Have mercy on us!' When he saw them, Jesus said, 'Go. Show yourselves to the priests.'"

"Didn't that hurt their feelings?" Ellie asked.

"I'm sure Jesus said it in a nice way, honey."

"So as they went off, the lepers realized that their skin condition had been healed, just like that. Isn't that cool?"

"I guess."

Children in the age of antibiotics and cortisone cream are not terribly impressed by the mere curing of a rash. "This was a big deal, girls," I say.

"But anyway, one of them, seeing that he was all better

and didn't have leprosy anymore, turned right around and went back to Jesus. He was praising God with a loud voice. He lay down at Jesus's feet . . ."—I don't know, Wooglet, I think that was polite back then—"and he said 'thank you.' And Jesus asked, 'Were not ten made clean?' "

"Why didn't he say 'You're welcome'?" asked Ellie, obviously developing a dim view of Jesus's manners.

"Fine. Jesus said, 'You're welcome, leper.'" And then he asked, 'Were not ten made clean? The other nine, where are they? Was none of them found to return, and give praise to God, except this foreigner?' Then he said to the man, 'Get up and go on your way. Your faith has made you well.' "

The girls got up and went on their way, joining their brothers and Bruce Willis in the playroom.

Theirs is an odd mother, who reads them creepy Bible miracle stories and goes tearing off to search for dead bodies in the woods at odd intervals. Lord knows what they are going to tell their shrinks someday, but for now, I should mention that they did remember to say, "Thank you for the story, Mom."

A miracle is generally understood to be an extraordinary event that cannot be explained by any plausible application of natural laws and principles. For example, there is no natural law or principle that permits a human being to stroll across the surface of the sea or to heal the sick with a word.

Most quotidian miracles are explainable in terms other than the supernatural. Trooper Tom Ballard's son Michael, for example, was given slim odds of survival. Born premature, he weighed just less than two pounds. He was no bigger than a couple of apples held in his father's hand and could wear his mother's wedding ring as a bracelet. But Michael happened to be born in a teaching hospital, one that had recently added an experienced and very talented neonatologist to its staff. Because he received excellent care made possible by the expensive, high-tech medical resources available in our day and place, Michael lived. His mom, Tonya, calls him her "miracle baby."

Perhaps all anyone means by the word *miracle* is an outcome that defies the odds. In a football game in which a Hail Mary pass is completed and the underdog wins, the victory is called a miracle. The conception of a child by an infertile couple, the complete remission of a notoriously lethal cancer, the appearance of a police officer just as a mugger pulls a knife . . . "What are the odds?" we ask, and call it a miracle.

So what are the odds of this?

On an ordinary weekday morning, a young woman named Christina left her dorm room at St. Mary's College in Waterford, Maine. She was planning to drive to Portland for a dental appointment and then to meet her mother for lunch.

A man was waiting in the parking lot—not for her, particularly, but for any one of the two thousand or so female undergraduates that might have appeared at that time and place. If Christina had fallen in that empty early-morning parking lot and been badly injured, and a man had happened to appear just in time to save her life, we would have called it a miracle.

But Christina did not fall, and the man who waited there did not save her life. He forced her into her vehicle, made her drive him to a remote area, then dragged her into the woods, raped her, tortured her, and took her life.

A miracle cannot simply be an event that is unlikely, for that would include the unlikely evil as well as the unlikely good. It cannot simply be an event inexplicable by natural law, for that would restrict use of the word to events that do not occur outside of stories. And even if we believe that Jesus smoothed the lepers' skin, made the blind man see, raised Jairus's daughter from the dead; even if we believe that each of Jesus's miracles actually took place, mere veracity does not lend them, or the word *miracle*, meaning. Scripture tells us, after all, that eyewitnesses to Jesus's miracles did not always find them meaningful.

The Sea of Galilee bears no footprints. The dead once raised are dead once more. The sighted blind no longer see. The skin of the lepers and the limbs of the lame are dust. However unlikely or impossible Jesus's deeds were once, they are all undone by now.

And Christina's murderer found her exactly where she needed to be for his purposes. He killed her, left her in a handy wood, and sauntered free.

Warden Rob Greenlaw and I were eating lunch in his truck a week or two after the St. Mary's College murder. He picked up his sandwich and held it in his hand, but didn't take a bite. He said, "I didn't have to see the body. Seeing the scene was bad enough. Just seeing where the body had been, where the vegetation was flattened down. Everybody there was pretty quiet. One of the state troopers found her sock. That was bad enough. It was more than bad enough."

He put the sandwich down, still unbitten. "I told Brianna . . . She's twelve, you know, and I didn't want to explain any of this to her. She's a little kid, for christsake. So I let her paint my toenails last night. And while she's painting my toenails, I told her, 'Sweetheart . . . make your stand right there in the parking lot. Do what you have to do, just *don't* get in the goddamned car.' "

After Christina's body was found, a state police detective telephoned the offices of the Department of Probation and Parole. She asked for a list of their clients in the area whose records and profiles suggested a capacity for violent sexual assault. Probation and parole provided a list of more than three hundred names.

"We are Legion," the demons sneered, when Jesus went to the territory of the Gerasenes to heal a man possessed by them (Mark 5:9). Three hundred men within an hour's drive of Waterford, Maine, could conceivably have committed this crime.

"It's one of those things you would really rather not know," Robby said, grinning slightly, as if his own refuge from this unwanted knowledge might be found in ironic humor; as if the devil he now knew might be transformed into a devil he doesn't know. He shrugged and the grin faded.

"My toenails are the color of Dubble Bubble," he said. "Don't tell anyone."

The young woman just happened to be in the St. Mary's parking lot at 7:30 a.m. that day. She didn't *have* to be in the parking lot: the dentist could have rescheduled, her mother could have taken her to lunch another day. She didn't *have* to be the victim. There was no necessity about this. She just happened to be there. And she just happened to be female.

The state police detective in charge of the case was also female—slender; dark hair; a pale, serious face. She wore a dark pantsuit, a detective's shield on her hip. Her name was Anna Love.

Within three days, the murderer was in custody. The investigation involved the usual diligent and determined retrieval and preservation of physical evidence, dogged tracking down of possible witnesses and interviews of same, complex interagency cooperation, and, once a prime suspect had been found, a skillful interrogation that resulted in a confession.

"Why did they let me out?" the murderer asked Detective Sergeant Love. "They should have kept me in jail, where I couldn't hurt anyone."

The Gerasene demoniac sought refuge among the tombs of a graveyard. Perhaps he, too, sought refuge from his own potential for evil; what harm could he do, what sins could he commit surrounded by those who were already dead?

For three days following Christina's murder, Detective Sergeant Love worked pretty much around the clock. In between all the meetings, the phone calls, the inspections of the scene and new pieces of physical evidence, the interviews with witnesses and family members, the interrogation of the suspect, and in between attending to the manifold legal requirements for proper documentation of all of the above, Anna would periodically duck into her office with her breast pump. Bottles of her milk would be sent home, where her husband waited with their baby.

If ours were a sensible culture, little girls would play with Anna Love action figures, badge in one hand, breast pump in the other.

"We are Legion," the demons said. The Department of Probation and Parole faxed a list. One man on the list did in fact commit this crime.

I wish Christina hadn't taken her last breath in the

presence of evil. I wish she wasn't afraid or in pain. Like Rob, I can find no distance, no mental compartment in which to hide from the cruelty of this death. Christina could be my daughter, my niece.

I remember walking across the dark quadrangle at Georgetown University, with the toothy points of my car keys poking out from between my fingers. They were supposed to be a weapon. I would try to visualize jabbing an assailant in the eyes with that fistful of keys. It bothered me then, and bothers me still, that instead of thinking about the lecture I had just attended or the paper I wanted to write or even about the cute, brown-eyed boy in the third row of the lecture hall, I was mentally preparing to take a stand in the parking lot. Young women are forced to waste a lot of time that way. I went to university in Washington, DC, a city known for its high crime rate. It would never have occurred to me, then or now, to hold my keys in my fist, prepared to fight off a murderer in small-town Maine at seven thirty in the morning.

Rob Greenlaw and I sit in the cab of his truck, picking at our lunches, wishing there had been a miracle for Christina, a miracle of a truly useful kind. We wish the killer had been healed in prison, the way Christ healed the Gerasene demoniac. Failing that, why couldn't he have slipped in the prison shower and banged his head hard? We wish ten leopards had appeared in the parking lot and chased the killer away, or a gaggle of early-morning Frisbee players had happened by in time. We wish the

Waterford cop had found the little car by the side of the road sooner and had made his way into the woods while there was still life in Christina's body. We wish Christina had survived.

But she did not survive. Her last breath left her lungs and was taken up by the trees. The killer departed, hitchhiked home to his mother's house over near Essex Junction. He took a shower. He watched TV.

Christina would not show up at the dentist's office, would not meet her mother for lunch, would not answer her cell phone. An alarm would be raised. At last, the Waterford cop would cautiously enter the woods beyond the abandoned car, look around until he glimpsed the sheen and pattern of Christina's jacket. He would approach her body, check for vital signs. He would make his way back to his cruiser, acutely aware of the feel of ordinary ground under the soles of his boots. He would press the button on his radio with his thumb, put his mouth to the mike, and call in the news.

And then they would come, my brethren. Hundreds of them from all over Maine would come streaming down highways and little roads, through villages, past farms and forests, shining lakes, bays with lobstermen at work. Swiftly, with their blue lights flashing, they would come.

They would diagram, photograph, and document the presence, position, and disposition of her body. They would enshroud it, lift it gently onto a stretcher, and carry it to the road where a hearse waited. More diagrams, more photographs. They would identify the path the murderer forced her to walk, the places where she struggled and was overcome; they would find the physical evidence of her last moments. More diagrams, more photographs. Everything they found could be used in court to convict the perpetrator, to give justice to Christina and her family. To the extent the law allows, they would succeed and brilliantly.

For me, Christina's restoration did not come in the arrest or in what happened in the courts to the man who committed this crime, however important and even grimly satisfying those things were in themselves. Instead, it was in the image of those dear and decent men—Rob, for example, with his quiet walk, his quiet way—moving with swift and loving purpose toward her body where it lay between the trees, bearing with them parenthood and friendship, grief and anger, order and care, and bearing beneath their badges their undefended hearts.

"We are Legion," the demon sneers.

No. *We* are legion.

These are the only miracles to be had in the story: the cops with their soft hearts breaking, and the fact that this violent sexual predator was nailed by a breastfeeding mother named Love—a righteous thing to contemplate there in the cab of Rob Greenlaw's truck.

From Jesus, ten lepers receive a cure. "And one of them, when he saw that he was healed, turned back, praising God with a loud voice. He prostrated himself at Jesus's feet and thanked him."

Were not ten made clean? Yes. Ten were made clean.

But only one received a miracle.

A miracle is not defined by an event. A miracle is defined by gratitude.

A string of coincidences stretching far back in human history converge to place a young woman in a parking lot at the very moment when a murderer happens by. A similar string of coincidences place a premature infant named Michael in a high-tech teaching hospital where a gifted doctor works to save him. Why? Why not?

Anything could happen, but only one thing will. If it is what we desire, what we long for so badly we feel it burning in our bones, if by chance this is given, we will fall on our grateful knees, praise God, and call it a miracle. And we will not be wrong.

"Your child yet lives," I said, and Mr. Moore's knees wobbled. A dog named Grace found her, awakened her with a cold nose, and Alison walked out of the wilderness. Her mother, laughing in her gratitude, called it a miracle.

All ten lepers were made clean; all ten went on to live whatever new life was afforded them thereby. We can be confident that all ten suffered other wounds, for life is wounding, and that all ten died, for life is also terminal. All ten have long since gone to dust and story. Sometimes the miracle is a life restored, but the restoration is always temporary. At other times, maybe most of the time, a miracle can only be the resurrection of love beside the unchanged fact of death.

"Don't drink and swim." "Wear a helmet." "Make your stand in the parking lot," I tell my children, as if I can hector them into a lifelong immunity from fear and pain. As a mother, I pray for miracles of the most ordinary kind on their behalf: I want their hearts to keep beating. I want them to live.

But then, a grateful heart beats in a world of miracles. If I could only speak one prayer for you, my children, it would be that your hearts would not only beat but grow ever greater in gratitude, that your lives, however long they prove to be and no matter how they end, continue to bring you miracles in abundance.

CHAPTER SEVENTEEN

I've never seen a fluffier snow than the snow that fell last night," Frank says.

It is a snow like feathers, snow so ill content to have fallen that it seeks every opportunity that breath, or breeze, or air displaced by a passing truck might offer to regain altitude and fly some more.

It's been a snowy season. Frank Gibney and I sit before a landscape painted and repainted white. A crow flies low over a field, its black wingtips elegantly angled upward. It is a gliding, black flourish on a white page.

"She was just under the ice," Frank says. "I took her out like this."

Windshield time: each of us, warden and chaplain, are looking forward at our parallel views of road, woods, snowy fields. The truck is parked in someone's driveway. We've been sitting here quite a while, sipping our Dunkin' Donuts coffee.

"I took her out just like this." Frank makes a cradling gesture with his arms.

Where is God in this? Frank is asking me. Not directly. Not in those words, but that is what he is asking, the same question my professors at seminary used to ask. Here it is, the good old theodicy issue: Why does evil exist? Why do the innocent suffer if God is good?

I've graduated from the seminary, been ordained, been working as a minister for a while now, a chaplain for nigh six years. I'd like to say I know what I'm doing, have ready answers for any questions that arise, but I don't. What I am conscious of is a softening in my body, an almost painful tenderness in my chest.

I didn't see the body of the little girl and saw the back of the mother only briefly; she was climbing into the ambulance with the body of her daughter when I arrived.

Adult drowning victims are often pronounced dead at the scene. Children who drown, particularly in very cold water, will be taken to the hospital and seen by a doctor before their death is officially declared. On rare occasions, children who have been under water for a considerable time have been known to revive. It didn't happen this time. The doctor had finished working on the little girl by the time Frank and I arrived at the hospital. The death officially occurred under halogen lights in the emergency room at Maine Medical Center. Frank was by the desk when he was told the child was gone.

But in my mind's eye, and perhaps in his own, Frank remained standing by the lakeshore. His boots were full of lake
water, his uniform sleeves and the front of his shirt, where it
bows out over his soft, late-middle-aged tummy, were soaked.
His arms were still bent to cradle the body of a drowned child.

"I found her mittens by the hole," Frank said. "Light mittens, not really warm enough for a day like this. They were
just polar fleece, but they were bright red. Couldn't miss 'em.
She must have taken them off, maybe thinking she could
grab onto the ice with her fingernails and pull herself out.
The water was only up to my waist, but it would have been
over her head. They called the dive team, but we didn't really
need them. I just broke a path through the ice, stomped
through with my boots. She was so light the ice held her, but
it wouldn't have held five pounds more, I don't think. Hell, if
she had worn thicker mittens, the ice wouldn't have held. But
it held long enough for her to get out over water too deep for
her to stand in. And then it broke."

"I pulled her out just like this," Frank says again, making the
cradling gesture with his wet arms. "God, she must have
been so cold. She must have been so scared."

Days later, I spoke to a group of colleagues: "The theological
challenge represented by the warden with the drowned child
is, I submit, one that a minister is not only invited to rise to
meet, but must rise to meet, rise and rise again to meet, if we

are to live in an authentic relationship with God." A group of ministers had met for a law enforcement breakfast in York County. There were maybe twenty of us there, including police officers, and I was the guest speaker. I now offer my retroactive apologies to my ministerial colleagues: You were eating your pancakes, and I told you a heartrending story. I'm sorry about that. Still, I was asked to tell you what I know, and this I know—the ice held until the child was out too far, until the water was over her head, then it broke. Though we are not in seminary, the question must still be asked: where was God in this?

Dear pastors, I can't make your answers to that question, however scripturally faithful, however tidy, match it. Warden Gibney was there with me at the breakfast, his cradling arms empty, his eyes full of tears.

Some game wardens are deeply and passionately Christian. Some are contentedly Catholic or Methodist. Some are skeptics or agnostics. Some try not to think about their faith until circumstances force the issue. A large number, perhaps even a majority, will say, I never really feel religious in church. When I was a little guy, I used to go to church, and I would stare out the window at the woods and fields, and watch the birds. That's where I still feel most religious, when I'm out in the woods.

Sometimes a warden says, very clearly and calmly, of a recent calamity (a drowning; an ATV accident; a man thrown from his snowmobile seventy feet into a stand of trees, where his body lodges in the snaggled arms of an oak): "This is all part of God's plan."

My role, in those moments, is to sit there in my black shirt and clerical collar, and hear him say it: "This is all part of God's plan."

Sometimes the same notion comes up very differently: "Hey, it's all part of God's plan, right?"

Frank said it with a snort of angry laughter. I waited. He said it again, this time as an urgent, angry question: "How the hell is this part of God's plan?"

It's only nine o'clock, the night is young and dark, my body soft and patient, the light snow swirling in the headlights. The truck is warm, and Dunkin' Donuts has a drive-through. We have a conversation.

My children asked me, "Why did Dad die?"

I told them, "It was an accident. There are small accidents, like knocking over your milk at the dinner table. And there are large accidents, like the one your dad was in. No one meant it to happen. It just happened. And his body was too badly damaged in the accident for his soul to stay in it anymore, and so he died.

"God does not spill milk. God did not bash the truck into your father's car. Nowhere in scripture does it say, 'God is car accident' or 'God is death.' God is justice and kindness, mercy, and always—always—love. So if you want to know where God is in this or in anything, look for love."

*   *   *

The death of the little girl with the red mittens is not God's will or plan. It is physics and biology, the bearing capacity of frozen water, the point at which hypothermia causes a small body's systems to fail. Don't look for God in the breaking ice or the dark water.

"Have you called home?" I ask Frank.

"Yeah," Frank answers. "I told my wife to give the grandkids extra smooches goodnight from their old poppy. They've been staying the night with us a lot lately. They're staying the night tonight. The thing is . . ." Frank said, then stopped.

Together we looked out through the windshield. We looked for a long time, easily ten minutes, before he finished the thought. "The thing is, I don't know what I would do if one of my girlies was killed," he says at last. "I'm too old. I don't think I could stand it."

Frank has two granddaughters, ages six and eight. Red is a common color for a child's pair of mittens. I move my hand over toward Frank. I don't actually touch him, I just put my hand closer to him on the bench seat, next to the packet of hand warmer, on top of the extra blaze orange hat he'd loaned me because I forgot mine.

"It would be hard," I say.

He nods, stares out the window. "I couldn't bear it."

"People would help you," I tell him.

He knows it's true. We, ourselves, are proof of that.

*   *   *

"I am willing to have the theodicy conversation with a cop, any cop—faithful or faithfree—not because he arrives at my answer, but because he has had to look suffering right in the face," I say to the clergy breakfast. "Whatever words he uses for God, he is still the one who had to take the little girl's body out of the water and see her face and hear her mother crying."

Here is my answer to the theodicy problem in a nutshell: Frank took the child out from under the ice with his own hands, tried to give her his breath, and his heart broke when he could not save her life. Frank *is* the answer.

Frank went home that night to his wife and his two little granddaughters. He gave all of them extra smooches, and when that wasn't enough, he carried the children, one at a time, into the room he shares with his wife. "All four of us in a double bed," he told me later.

"Cozy," I said.

"Oh yeah," he said. "I had all my girlies 'round me and the heat cranked up. Here it is, December, and we woke up sweating, but I slept."

CHAPTER EIGHTEEN

On June 12, 2004, I was ordained a Unitarian Universalist minister. My first official act was to pray for the game wardens and other law enforcement officers present.

I was sorely tempted to offer prayers for a guarantee of safety. What prayer springs to mind when I hear one of them on the radio, headed off to something that sounds a little scary? *Oh God, please protect him. Oh God, please keep her safe.*

On the other hand, if safety were a police officer's top priority, she would doubtless have chosen another profession. To be truly safe would require that she set aside her own calling, terminate her own loving service to God and neighbor.

So I could not ask God to protect their bodies—though please, guys, do your best to protect your own, won't you?

"Join me as you will . . ." I said.

"May you be granted capable and amusing comrades, observant witnesses, and gentle homecomings.

"May you be granted respite from what you must know of human evil, and refuge from what you must know of human pain.

"May God defend the goodness in your hearts.

"May God defend the sweetness in your souls . . ."

On an ordinary Wednesday evening in early 1996, my three-year-old daughter, Woolie, was climbing up my back, clutching a wet, half-chewed green apple in her fist. "It's me," she said, when she reached my face. She gave me an apple-juicey smooch, and crushed the apple gently against my forehead.

My husband was in the bathroom, loudly exhorting the toilet to swallow his turd without choking.

"You can do it!" he was saying. "I believe in you!"

Hearing me giggle, he played it out: "Y'hear that? She's laughing at you. She's dissin' you, man! She thinks you can't do this. Show the woman what you're made of, man! That's right. Do it! That's right!"

Old house, small pipes, wacky husband, laughing wife. My daughter rolled on the bed, hooting with glee, because she was the youngest of four and wanted to be in on everything.

How does one speak of such happiness or gratitude? I wrote the words in my journal: "I am in love with Drew."

We had been married for almost eleven years—thirteen years, if you count living in sin. We lived most of that time together in Maine, most of it in the same house I live in now. Every time I drive south, I pass over the bridge where he died, the bridge that is now named after him. "Hello, Dad!" the children holler, their voices following the river as it travels downstream. The river passes the bench by the lighthouse where we scattered Drew's ashes; it will carry our greetings on to the sea.

Drew is present everywhere—in my home, in my work, in my heart. He is present in the very landscape I inhabit. This makes my world friendlier as well as sacred.

For my in-laws, our house, the bridge, the sidewalks and shops, the firehouse, the café, the bookstore, the whole of Thomaston and perhaps the whole state of Maine remains a place of fearsome pain, even after all these years. For them, I think, it is set apart as the place Drew died. It's not because they are peculiarly mournful or incapable of "getting on with life." It's just that they don't live here.

I was in the high school gymnasium in Thomaston not too long ago. It's your basic, sixties-era gym, with a wood floor, basketball hoops, and a stage that gets set up for the performance of musicals, for graduation, and, in 1996, for the funeral of a Maine state trooper.

With a thousand or more police officers slated to attend, there were far more mourners than any of the churches in the area could accommodate. So inmates from the prison mowed the lawns, tidied the grounds, and set up risers for the choirs. The basketball hoops were hoisted out of the way, and the stage was brightened with flowers. Out on the soccer field, a lone trumpet player waited for the signal to play taps.

Drew's funeral is a vivid memory, one I carry with me

every time I go into the gym. And I go there pretty often. I go there for Peter's basketball games, to chaperone school dances, and to attend the larger town meetings. I gave the commencement address for the class of 1999 there. I've eaten lasagna at a fundraising supper there, and on that stage I've watched Zach play a silly sot in the musical *Guys and Dolls*.

Every time I go into that ordinary gymnasium, the memory of Drew's funeral becomes more deeply embedded in layers of other memories attached to the same space. The painful memory is not obscured or buried. It is placed in the context of continuing life: my own life, the lives of my children, the continuing life of the community.

For the children and me and for Drew's local friends, Thomaston is a bastion of ordinary life. Even Mr. Moss's funeral home, the ornate Victorian edifice where Drew's body was prepared and where it lay during the week of the funeral, has more than that memory connected with it. Mr. and Mrs. Moss make their home around the back of the building. On Halloween night, the children walk up the driveway past the parked hearse, the same vehicle that took their father's body to the crematory. They go to the kitchen door, where Mrs. Moss waits with popcorn balls. "Trick or treat," they holler.

The bridge where Drew died is not just a memorial to him. It is also a bridge between the towns of Thomaston and Warren.

Years ago, I buried a dog with my own hands. I made her a bed of flowers: Queen Anne's lace, daisies, soft blue cornflowers. Cavemen did as much: evidence of ancient flowers has been found beside the remains of the ancient dead. Beautiful floral bodies have always gone prematurely to the tomb, like the young women thrown upon the funeral pyres of Viking chieftains. It is a strange, human reflex to sacrifice the living for the dead.

Because she was a dog, not a human being, Cornelia's death and burial were simple and immediate experiences. I handled her body, I dug the hole in the earth, I put her body into it, and I covered her. Flowers, dirt, stones. Until relatively recently, this is pretty much the way the physical remains of beloved human beings were handled too.

Mourning, that excruciating conspiracy of human memory and human love, demands rituals that can prolong the relationship between the living and the dead. Even protecting Cornelia's body from buzzards was a peculiarly human concern. What difference did it make to her whether birds shared the worms' dinner?

Drew's body was remarkably undamaged in the accident that killed him. My mother, Drew's good friend Tom Ballard, two state police sergeants, and I bathed his body and dressed it in his uniform. We cried the whole time we did it, when we weren't laughing. It is what Drew would have done for me or for any of us. It was important, and it was lovely.

Later, his family and friends accompanied Drew's body to the crematory in Portland. We cried all that day too, when we weren't laughing. It was another stone placed, with care, upon his grave.

Drew's body went where all bodies—my body, your body—will eventually go. Like the bodies of Mr. Levesque, poor Betsy, and the little girl with the red mittens, we will all go into the dirt to become the dirt that welcomes those who come next.

The state named the bridge Drew died on after him. There's a garden dedicated to his memory at Merryspring Park in Camden, a bench at Peopleplace Cooperative Preschool, another at the lighthouse in Port Clyde where his ashes were scattered. There are two scholarship funds named after him. The Live Poets Society dedicated their annual anthology to him. I'm writing about him right now. These are stones on his grave too.

Faced with a significant loss, we might spend years piling and repiling stones, grooming the grave, contesting the will, making rooms, houses, whole lives into shrines.

I suppose at some point this becomes unhealthy. It is an unnecessary waste of a human life to fling it onto a funeral pyre or to make of it a stone.

In traditional cultures, the rituals of mourning are strictly, and perhaps comfortingly, preordained. Jewish Law, for example, sets aside a full year for mourning the death of a parent. That twelve-month period is demarked at psychologically astute intervals of decreasing intensity—seven days, thirty days—with various rituals and requirements until, at last, the veil is removed from the tombstone and the year is up. Mourning is complete, and, while the dead are not forgotten, life is now emphatically the business of the living.

In the abstract, this might seem confining, insensitive to

the individual mourner for whom a year might be too much or too little time for grief. Still, there is much wisdom in it, distilled as it's been over generations of intimate experience with death. I have to say that when Drew died, it might have been very useful to have had a widely accepted and understood blueprint to follow for my widowhood. Instead, there was a bewildering plethora of options and choices, from how to dispose of Drew's body to when I might begin dating. How could I know which stones or how many stones to place upon the grave? How can any of us know when enough is enough?

Someday, the last stone must be placed, and we must walk away, but when? I think if I were my own minister, I would answer that question this way, and I won't pretend it isn't hard:

Go ahead. Arrange and rearrange the stones on top of your beloved's grave. Keep arranging those stones for as long as it hurts to do it, then stop, just before you really want to.

Put the last stone on and walk away.

Then light your candles to the living. Say your prayers for the living. Give your flowers to the living. Leave the stones where they are, but take your heart with you. Your heart is not a stone. True love demands that, like a bride with her bouquet, you toss your fragile glass heart into the waiting crowd of living hands and trust that they will catch it.

CHAPTER NINETEEN

The worst death notification any of us can remember, the one that stays with us and keeps us up at night, is this one: On a dark winter afternoon, in a living room filled with people, we uttered the usual words, "I'm sorry to have to tell you this, but John Smith has been killed in a snowmobile accident." The answer was a long, blank stare. Then the dead man's brother said, "He was an asshole. When can we have his snowmobile?"

Hell is when you die, and no one cares.

When I teach death notification to new wardens at Maine Criminal Justice Academy, I tell them to expect the newly widowed, childless, friendless, or loverless to wail and cry, to fall down on the ground, to gnash their teeth, perhaps to vomit or eliminate.

"This is love," I say. "It's just love.

"Thank God for the blessing of breaking hearts, the

blessing of mourning, the blessing of being, and the blessing of being in love."

One afternoon, my daughters and I sat in the playroom compiling a list of the attributes the next man in our lives should have. A relationship with a man my children had come to love and trust had recently ended, leaving us all feeling betrayed and abandoned, shocked and distressingly suspicious. Woolie was grimly determined that we should take no chances henceforth.

"A boyfriend has to be funny," Ellie offered, as Woolie took up her pad of paper and pencil. Woolie assented, and wrote it down.

"He has to tell the truth," she added, still scribbling. "Is there an *h* in *honest*?"

"Put down that he has to have been married before," I said. "And he must have children."

"Children?" Woolie squawked. "What about us?"

"We would have to put up with stepsiblings," Ellie said doubtfully, "and they would have to put up with us."

"No babies," said Woolie.

"Okay, no babies. But I'm telling you, he needs to be a father. Then he will know what being a parent feels like. He will understand how wildly and devotedly I love you."

"That makes sense," Ellie said. "Can his kids be girls? I have enough brothers."

Zach, who was getting a glass of milk from the refrigerator, poked his head in the playroom long enough to declare that he had enough sisters too.

I was warming to the fantasy by this time. "And along with kids, he has to have a job that helps people. Whatever his profession, he should *serve*."

"Like your job?"

"Yeah, but he doesn't have to be a minister. In fact, he probably shouldn't be a minister."

"We have enough religion around this house," Ellie agreed.

"So he could be a doctor or something," I said. "Most kinds of doctors are okay. And certain kinds of lawyers."

"A prosecutor," Zach hollered from the other room. (That's a cop's son for you.)

Peter, coming in from outdoors, caught the gist of the conversation. "How about a guy who owns a business? Some really altruistic sort of businessman, like Paul Newman."

"Paul Newman would be okay," I said judiciously.

"Or maybe a teacher," Ellie said. "Or a police officer or a game warden."

"Nope. Can't be a game warden."

"Why not? I like game wardens," Woolie protested.

"I like game wardens too, but I'm not allowed to date them."

"Really? Is that a law?"

"It's not a law. It's called ministerial ethics."

"I don't see what ethics has to do with it," Ellie said. "If you and a game warden fall in love, what's unethical about that?"

"If I become a game warden's girlfriend—let alone, God forbid, his ex-girlfriend . . . then that game warden wouldn't have his chaplain anymore. And his friends wouldn't either. I'd be something else to them, someone they like or don't like, but not their minister. I can't risk taking a warden's chaplain away from him, even by falling in love."

"That's too bad," Woolie said. "Game wardens are handsome."

"They are indeed."

We were silent for a little while, mulling over the tremendous sacrifices God demands of God's servants. "But could you marry another kind of police officer?"

"Sure," I said.

"Or a firefighter?"

"Yup. And let's say this too: If he doesn't have a job helping people, if he is a bureaucrat or a businessman (other than Paul Newman), then he has to have a *really serious* hobby that has to do with service to human beings. The service is important, because if he doesn't serve, he won't understand why I do my work."

"He should vote," Ellie said suddenly. "Voting matters."

Woolie wrote it down. "And even if he isn't a minister, he has to go to church," she said, "because you are a minister, and he has to be interested in what you do."

Wise girl.

I have plenty of friends who don't attend church (more who don't than do, as a matter of fact), but the ideal husband, we decided, would have a more natural understanding not only of why I do my work, but also why I am what I am. So Woolie carefully wrote "attends church" down on her list.

"Funny, honest, has been married, has children, serves, votes, attends church," she read. "How's that?"

"Terrific," I said.

Woolie taped the list to the refrigerator for easy reference and went off to practice her cello. Ellie remained behind, pondering. Ellie is inclined to ponder.

"That list describes Dad," she said wistfully.

"Yes, it does," I said.

We didn't ask to have Drew back. We knew better than that by then. Neither did we ask that the next man be handsome or creative. We didn't demand an excellent cook, an educated reader, a lover of art or books or travel. We didn't ask that he speak other languages or avoid television or understand teenagers. When the girls and I sent our little personal ad into the ether, we didn't even request that his children be interesting or that they be lovable and love us in return. We asked only the minimum from a parsimonious God. We didn't know that we could ask for Simon.

Once, in conversation with a very nice Baptist classmate at the seminary, I admitted that if Drew hadn't died I probably would never have become a minister.

"You see!" she responded brightly. "God knew what he was doing!"

This is the sort of remark that, however common, makes me despair of Christianity's ability to respond in any helpful or sensible way to the reality of death.

"Surely, God was not so urgently in need of Unitarian Universalist ministers that he needed to kill a father of four in order to make one?" I retorted in what was probably an unnecessarily icy voice.

Death alters the reality of our lives; the death of an intimate changes it completely. No part of my life, from my most ethereal notions of God to the most mundane detail of tooth brushing, was the same after Drew died. Life consisted of one rending novelty after another, as anyone who has lost a spouse can attest.

Still, as time went on, some of those novelties proved to be blessings. And, like anyone who has survived the death of an intimate, I had to learn to live with a paradox. If Drew had lived, I would not have gone to seminary, would not be ordained, would not have become the warden service chaplain. There are places that would have gone unvisited and friends I would never have met, friends I now can't imagine doing without. So while on one hand there is my darling Drew, whom I will never cease to love and never cease to long for, on the other hand, there is a wonderful life that I enjoy and am grateful for.

I can't make those two realities—what I've lost and what I've found—fit together in some tidy pattern of divine causality. I just have to hold them on the one hand and on the other, just like that.

As it happens, not as it was planned but as it turned out, this is my life. It now includes my beloved, a man named

Simon. He is handsome and creative, an excellent cook. He reads. He speaks French and Dutch. He doesn't have a television. And he is the father of Jacobus and Ilona, two (count 'em!) teenage children who are interesting and bright, lovable and loving. Simon is a funny, honest man who votes and serves. He goes to church. I love him, and he, by grace, loves me.

Chapter Twenty

On my way to Presque Isle for a search, I spied a coyote trotting purposefully across the far end of a freshly plowed field. Coyotes are wary of humans and smart. I'd never gotten a good look at a live one before.

An antique, stuffed specimen sits in the hallway at the warden service's Division A headquarters. Its back and shoulders are gray, the ruff of fur around the taxidermied throat is a yellowish cream. One day an older warden caught me patting its stiff, flat head. The gesture must have looked more apologetic than affectionate.

"You don't have to feel bad," he said gently. "That dog'd be dead by this time anyhow."

Division A's stuffed coyote is about the size, though not the shape, of a Springer spaniel. The live coyote out in the field looked to be the size of a big shepherd. Or maybe a wolf.

There were other cars traveling down the road, but she must have sensed, somehow, that I was slowing down for a better look. The coyote was at least three hundred yards away, but she turned her head and looked pointedly in my direction. I was overdue at the command post, but I couldn't resist pulling over and rolling down my window. When my car stopped, the coyote stopped too. Across an expanse of dark earth awaiting seed, we regarded one another. The damp air held the wild, sweet scent of loam.

You're so far away, I thought. *I wonder if I could convince Edna that a chaplain must be equipped with a good set of binoculars?*

The coyote stood very still, watching me, her ears pricked.

"How do you know I'm looking at you?" I whispered, and, as if she'd heard, the coyote turned and vanished into the woods.

"Dear Brother," I e-mailed. "I think one reason I like working with crisis and death is that all the complicated and complicating tools of our natal tribe—the intellect, rational analysis, the all-pervasive irony—all these are useless.

"It doesn't matter how educated, moneyed, or smart you are: when your child's footprints end at the river's edge, when the one you love has gone into the woods with a bleak outlook and a loaded gun, when the chaplain is walking toward you with bad news in her mouth, then only the clichés are true, and you will repeat them, unashamed. Your life, too, will swing suddenly and cruelly in a new direction with breathtaking speed, and if you are really wise—and it's surprising and wondrous, Brother, how many people have this wisdom in them—you will know enough to look around for love. It will be there, standing right on the hinge, holding out its arms to you. If you are wise, whoever you are, you will let go, fall against that love, and be held."

When it was my turn, I fell against it—against love—and was held.

My friend Monica was with me, her arms wrapped around me. Drew's family had been notified. My parents and siblings were flying toward Maine. And the news was trickling out, already, into the community: casseroles were being assembled.

Through the isosceles triangle formed by Monica's elbows, through the front windows of my house, I caught a glimpse of the river where it flowed past town at the bottom of Knox Street. The same river flowed beneath the bridge on which Drew died. His last views were of the dark pines of his adopted state, the stones, and the shining water. The cool bright air, washed clean by snow, made way for the final gestures of Drew's dear hands and accepted his last breath.

I took in the same air, saw the sun on the same water. I felt my friend Monica's arms around me. Her soft body was planted right there, right on the hinge of my life.

The Episcopal priest arrived. He wore a black shirt, a Roman collar. The white vinyl boomerang of his calling glowed against his throat like a flame.

So I showed up, not so long ago, in a small northern Maine community. An elderly woman, an Alzheimer's patient—let's call her Corinne—had wandered off, and the PLS was near the woods.

The wardens established a command post at the fire station, and by the time I got there, it was swarming with men and women in green uniforms. Ron Dunham was there, dogless and alone, mourning Grace. She had recently contracted cancer and been reluctantly euthanized. Alex Hatch had been promoted to sergeant; he wore his new stripes self-consciously. Frank Gibney was there, and Don Carpenter showed up with his dog, Tiki. He took me aside to tell me the exciting news that his foster son's adoption had gone through. "He's ours now, for real," Don said cheerfully. "Can you believe it?"

Hannah Robitaille wanted to know if I'd heard the one about the church lady who goes to the L.L.Bean housewares department wanting to buy monogrammed guest towels for the First Unitarian Church of Kennebunkport, Maine. "Think about it," she said.

Nate Robertson and the overhead team had their laptops and maps organized, teams had already been sent forth with GPS units. A small army of volunteers was assembling at the firehouse, eager to assist the wardens in their search.

Some of the volunteers could lay claim to a certain level of applicable expertise. There were emergency service providers of various kinds: local firefighters, off-duty sheriff's deputies and town cops, and woods-savvy members of the local rod and gun club. The volunteer Maine search and rescue dog teams, those middle-aged hobbyists with their fine, trained dogs, had arrived in force.

Then there were the less obviously skilled: A half dozen elderly backwoods guys in torn flannel shirts, a gaggle of college students with unfortunate piercings, some overweight Elks, and a Shriner or two. The members of a local equestrien club appeared with their horses. Also present were the owner of a stained-glass studio and her domestic partner; a retired state trooper; and a state senator with his teenage daughter in tow.

The high school varsity soccer team abandoned its late-summer practice to came out to search, along with a bunch of U.S. Marines who had been cooling their heels in Bangor, awaiting transshipment to Iraq. And, arriving in a van with wire-mesh reinforced windows and under the direct supervision of a guard, was a group of men in neon yellow shirts, inmates from the Downeast Correctional Facility, a prison primarily though not exclusively reserved for sex offenders.

Corinne's son, Jim, able-bodied and fiftyish, announced that searching the woods for his mom would be less stressful than just sitting around waiting. So Jim was put on a team as well.

Those members of the community too old or obviously out-of-shape to search set up shop in the firehouse kitchen and commenced to cooking.

The wardens gave each search team a map and an area to search. Each team had a xeroxed photograph of Corinne, a white-haired lady smiling vaguely at the camera. Each team had a handheld GPS unit, so their movements would be precisely recorded. The search dogs would go into the woods to nose the rich air, seeking the signature flavors of human life or human death. The horses would clip-clop along the railroad bed, their riders' high vantage point giving them a nice view down into the shrubbery on either side. Local teens on ATVs would roar up and down the dirt roads and logging trails. Foot searchers would spend the morning hacking through deadfall and bogs, working their way in long, slow lines across blueberry barrens and along cliff edges and riverbanks.

It was hard going. The terrain was rough. The weather turned ugly. Rain fell, and still they searched. Everyone wanted to find the woman in the picture. Even those who had never met her wanted to find her. Through the very effort of searching for her, they had begun to love her a little, to love Corinne, the mother of Jim. At the very least, they wanted to know what had become of her.

Perhaps you would like to fast-forward to the end of the story. Was Corinne, the white-haired woman, found, and found alive?

Well, usually, there is a find. The wardens work hard to get one, and generally they succeed. But I'm not going to tell you if it happened in this case, for in the end this is not a story about success, however richly deserved and deeply desired such success might be. The truth is that while usually there is a find, sometimes there isn't. Sometimes the wardens, the searchers, the family members—heroes all—must go home without success, without even an explanation of how the failure happened. That's hard.

In a true story, the end is never tidy. So I can only give you untidy searchers returning to the firehouse for their lunch. They are tired, cold, and very hungry. They are greeted with platters of lasagna, bowls of coleslaw, tottering piles of oatmeal cookies, and jiggling, jewel-colored Jell-O salads. The odor of damp boots and wet dogs mingles with the scents of fish chowder and fresh biscuits.

When the prisoners from the Downeast Correctional Facility come into the command post to hand in their GPS units, Nate Robertson meets them at the door. He puts his hand on one neon yellow shoulder: "Weren't you guys with us on the Addison search?" he asks. The man nods, shyly. "You guys were great. Thanks for coming."

Jim comes back to the firehouse with a heavy heart. He has scratches on his cheek, twigs in his hair, pine needles down his pants, and his mother is still nowhere to be found. Yet he takes in the scene before him, mops the rain from his face, and smiles.

"Look at this," he says. "Look at this! This is *incredible.*"

The firehouse is filled with people. The old coots in flannel shirts, the middle-aged dog handlers, and the college students with piercings are sharing American chop suey with the state senator and his teenage daughter. The U.S. Marines are comparing blisters with the soccer players, the sheriff's deputies are breaking bread with the convicts, game wardens share Jell-O with equestrians, the stained-glass artist offers the retired state trooper an oatmeal cookie.

In a little while, they will go back out and search some

more. They will try to find a body, living or dead. For now, they are here together, joined in community, bent on the common purpose of love.

"Everyone in the world is here," the lost woman's son exclaims. "It's a miracle!"

Amen.

Reading Group Guide

A conversation with Kate Braestrup

How has living in a family of eight people influenced your writing?

Left to myself, I would probably write more, and faster. On the other hand, when left to myself I become moody and peculiar. I forget to eat. I fail to notice that the car is making a horrible grinding noise. I suspect dental floss of being a marketer's hoax rather than a true requirement of good hygiene.

Luckily, owing to various biological urges we need not examine here, I am surrounded by human beings whose own moods and peculiarities call forth my more sensible instincts. Because I love them, I am irrationally devoted to their good nutrition and automotive safety, and this has a salubrious spillover effect: living with a family of eight people probably keeps me alive and sane, prerequisites (one assumes) for writing well.

Do you have a writing routine?

I don't have a routine for anything. If I could have a routine, it would consist of lying in bed until at least ten in the morning, every morning. I would knit, doodle in my journal, and pretend to be thinking profound thoughts, while my husband shushes the children, holds my calls, and brings me coffee. Then I might drift over to my studio and write brilliant prose, while the aforementioned husband brings me delicious treats at appropriate intervals throughout the day.

Believe it or not, some days really do go this way, but as a mother and as chaplain to the Maine Warden Service, I'm on call pretty much all the time. Neither familial nor Maine woodland calamities seem to happen according to schedule.

I wrote a novel, *Onion,* when my children were babies, and so I was trained to write when the opportunity presented itself and to drop the work and walk away when a squawk was heard. I've never had my life set up in such a way that all I am doing is writing. I don't know what would happen if I did.

You have lived in many different places. What is it about Maine that makes it special to you?

My father was a foreign correspondent for the *New York Times* and then the *Washington Post,* so my early childhood was spent in Algiers, Paris, and Bangkok. Even after coming back to the States, we moved every five years or so. My extended family spent summers in Maine, so the state remained a geographic constant in an otherwise peripatetic childhood. My first husband, Drew, and I moved to Maine in

1986, and by the time he died, I had finally been living in one place long enough to feel safely at home.

Maine has many wonderful features, as many other writers and artists have noted. We've got plenty of outdoor recreation, adorable New England architecture, and scenery out the wazoo. But Maine also has people who have not forgotten how to function within a community. Having been on the receiving end of community care when I really needed it, I have become a student of the art, and Maine proves a fine school.

You are also the author of a novel, Onion. *How different was the process of writing a memoir?*

Writing *Onion* let me know that I was in fact capable of the sort of sustained attention and sheer effort that producing a book-length work requires. I also knew that publication was possible, because I had done it once before.

The big difference between writing one and the other has more to do with experience than with genre. I was so much younger when I wrote *Onion* that, while I was driven to write something, it wasn't clear what higher purpose I was serving. My motivation in writing *Here If You Need Me* was much clearer: I was called not only to put words on paper, but to tell the truth in love. The one question I had for my early readers wasn't "How's the structure?" or "Does it read well?" but "Does this book feel loving to you?" If and when I again write fiction, this motive would remain. "All that I ever hope to say in books is that I love the world," said E. B. White, and that about sums it up.

Questions and topics
for discussion

1. Kate Braestrup admits that before serving as chaplain to the Maine Warden Service, she had little idea of what the position entailed, joking that people asked her: "What does a warden service chaplain do? Bless the moose?" (page 62). Did you know the role that game wardens play prior to reading *Here If You Need Me*? If you found yourself in a situation that required the warden service's intercession, would you want the assistance of a chaplain?

2. In the Author's Note at the beginning of the book, Braestrup writes that her favorite definition of the Greek word *logos* is "story." Of the many stories Kate tells in the book relating to her role as warden service chaplain, which was your favorite?

3. When Kate Braestrup was a child, she believed she experienced a vision of Jesus Christ from her family's car, only to find a few days later that what she had seen was a fiberglass statue placed in a memorial garden. Have you ever had a similar, seemingly inexplicable experience? Like Kate, did you eventually find the explanation?

4. Braestrup writes: "I love my uniform. Quite apart from whatever unwholesome sartorial fetish this may reflect, my uniform is so *useful*" (page 64). Do you share a similar feeling about some aspect of your profession? If so, what is the source or cause of the attachment?

5. Although Drew was employed as a Maine state trooper, Kate writes that he had planned to begin a second "career" as a minister. Have you ever considered changing professions? Given the opportunity, what new occupation would you choose?

6. Upon Kate's decision to become an ordained minister, her brother writes to her expressing his skepticism about religion. How are these e-mail exchanges important to Kate in terms of how she regards her own faith?

7. At one point Braestrup writes: "That's where I still feel most religious, when I'm out in the woods" (page 186). Discuss the role nature plays in *Here If You Need Me*, especially as it affects both Braestrup's profession and her faith.

8. Near the memoir's end, Braestrup writes: "I can't make those two realities—what I've lost and what I've found—fit together in some tidy pattern of divine causality. I just have to hold them on the one hand and on the other, just like that" (page 202). Does the conclusion Braestrup reaches make sense to you?

9. At one point Braestrup offers proof that God has a sense of humor. Despite the tragic events described in *Here If You Need Me*, the memoir encompasses many humorous moments as well. How does humor serve Kate and the wardens she works with in their professional capacities? What was your favorite funny moment?